ALLIANCE FOR CHANGE

A Plan
for Community Action
on Adolescent Drug Abuse

James F. Crowley

Community Intervention, Inc.

Contributing writers: Joe Muldoon, Pam Eyden
Editors: Kathleen Michels, Mary Lou Kosar
Illustrations: Roger Boehm
Cover photograph: Jerry Taube
Typesetting: Offset Compositors, Inc.

Copyright © 1984, 1989 by Community Intervention, Inc.
All rights reserved.

Reproduction in whole or in part, in any form, including storage in a memory device system, is forbidden without written permission of Community Intervention, Inc.

ISBN 0-9613416-0-2
Library of Congress Catalog Number 84-071356

Inquiries, orders, and catalog requests should be addressed to:
  Community Intervention, Inc.
  529 South Seventh Street, Suite 570
  Minneapolis, MN 55415
  Call Toll Free 800-328-0417
  In Minnesota, call 612-332-6537

Printed in the United States of America

To my loving daughter, Kiersten

Her patience gave me time, her maturity gave me strength, and her love and sense of humor gave me hope. When my days were filled with work, she played by my side; when her days were filled with disappointments, she shared her pain without punishing. Kiersten's understanding, cooperation, and support have allowed me to finish this and dozens of other projects. We have come a long way together.

Contents

Acknowledgments xiii

Introduction 1

Part One 5

Chapter One **A Time of Reaction** 7

8 Dramatic but futile approaches: crackdowns on paraphernalia sellers—apprehension of "pushers"—undercover police operations—use of police dogs—the "show-biz" approach ■ **19 The pendulum effect:** adults' role in the problem ■ **22 The need for balance**

Chapter Two **Changing the Game Plan** 25

26 The need for agreement: the drug alcohol—a range of problems, a range of intervention techniques—problems related to use not sole criterion for intervention—priority for action versus primary problem—no need to compromise ■ **33 General strategies for community mobilization:** networking—community intervention—the intervention-to-prevention approach

Chapter Three **Barriers to Action, Components of Change** 45

   47 **Common barriers:** delusion, denial, and fear—blaming—a narrow perspective—good drugs, bad drugs—good kids, bad kids—promises, promises—ain't it a shame? ■ **59 Key components of effective programming:** awareness and education—identification and referral—counseling and treatment—support groups and activities—incorporation of key program components into various systems

Chapter Four **Mobilizing for Action** 75

   76 **Mobilization step by step:** step one: form an interest group—step two: focus on appropriate goals—step three: convert the interest group into a task force—step four: train task force members—step five: gain formal recognition for the task force—step six: set the task force agenda—step seven: do a needs assessment—step eight: write a program proposal—step nine: obtain financial support—step ten: present the program proposal ■ **100 Need for patience and perseverance**

Chapter Five **Focus on School Drug Programs** 103

   106 **Rationale for schools' involvement:** schools' role in early intervention ■ **110 Early-intervention programming** ■ **111 Internal organization:** the core team—the program coordinator—the advisory board ■ **120 Confidentiality:** confidentiality versus discretion—discretion versus advocacy of "responsible" use—important but nonconfidential information—effects of being too confidential—information sharing on need-to-know basis only

Chapter Six **School Program Dynamics**   127

    127 Awareness and education: target groups—basic content of presentations—content development and delivery ▪ **136 Identification and referral:** schools' role in identifying drug problems—need for clear-cut policies and procedures—practical identification and referral procedures—insight groups ▪ **147 Counseling and treatment** ▪ **148 Support:** schools' role in providing support—support for children of alcoholics ▪ **153 Summary of school-based programming** ▪ **154 Program evaluation**

Part Two   157

Chapter Seven **Success in Ohio and Montana**   159

    159 The Ohio story: superintendents lead the way: a call to action—the Regional Council on Alcoholism—communitywide involvement—creation of services—statewide action ▪ **164 Dynamics of the Ohio story:** public, united, top-level support—shared responsibility—start-up funds from an outside source—action, not just awareness—temporary use of out-of-state services—judicious use of consultants—large-scale training effort ▪ **167 The Montana story: parents organize a grass-roots movement:** pressure from parents—the business connection—proliferation of training workshops—development of school-based programs—administrators' participation in training—volunteer support—changes in juvenile court systems—special training a priority for helping professionals ▪ **173 Analysis of the Montana story:** parents, a powerful pressure group—risk taking by the private sector—training, a mandatory first step

Chapter Eight **Spotlight on Individual Efforts** 177

177 Parents groups: rescuing kids from the fast lane ■ **180 Community volunteers:** gathering momentum for a community campaign ■ **182 School counselors:** doing it right from the beginning—creating effective agents of change ■ **186 Program coordinators:** building programs one step at a time—keeping the lines of communication open—closing loopholes in policies and procedures ■ **194 Social service professionals:** developing skills, then letting go ■ **197 Probation officers:** offering a promising alternative

Appendixes **201**

201 Selected sources of information ■ **203 Sample surveys of drug use patterns** ■ **215 Sample form for needs assessment interview** ■ **217 Sample information form on service providers** ■ **219 Sample program proposal outline** ■ **223 References**

About the Author **225**

Acknowledgments

This book would never have become a reality if its preparation had been left to me alone. As it was, many individuals directly or indirectly made important contributions. Although I can do no more than scratch the surface, I wish to acknowledge with warm appreciation—

- The 50 consultants who make up the Community Intervention, Inc., training team. Given their cumulative expertise garnered from every system in the community and their special focus on adolescent drug use, they have kept our approach on the cutting edge. Equally important, they have presented our approach with consummate care and skill to concerned people throughout the country.
- The thousands of educators, parents, volunteers, students, and helping professionals from all fields who have attended our training events. Through hard work and dedication, they are putting our concepts to work in their own systems and communities, thus transforming theory into practice. In the midst of their efforts, many have generously taken the time to give us feedback so that we could share their practical experiences with others.
- The office staff who, with very little public recognition, are committed to our approach and hold the organization together while the training team travels around the country.
- My family and friends whose trust in and support of me and Community Intervention, Inc., have been unquestioning and

constant. Their devotion and caring have allowed this organization and its philosophy to evolve beyond our greatest expectations.

Of equal importance are some specific individuals to whom I wish to pay special tribute for their contributions to this book. First and foremost is Joe Muldoon. He is personally responsible for almost everything written at Community Intervention, Inc., which truly makes him indispensable. He adopted this project as his own and put countless hours and matchless care into developing many of the core ideas expressed in this book. I am also indebted to Pam Eyden for her major contribution as a writer. Her unique ability allowed her to bring order and sense to my ideas and scribblings. Kathleen Michels and Mary Lou Kosar's invaluable editing of this book made it eminently more readable than it otherwise would have been. Another prime contributor was Roger Boehm, who so creatively illustrated many of the concepts all of us here are striving to communicate effectively. Last but not least, Dolly Gove was there throughout the lengthy writing and editing process to type and retype the manuscript. I am deeply indebted to all of these individuals and to many others too numerous to mention. To all of you I say a very sincere "Thank you."

Introduction

Alliance for Change is for *you* if you are—

- a PARENT who is angry and frightened because so many adults in your community seem to accept as inevitable the use of alcohol and other drugs by teenagers and seem no longer to believe that young people have a right to play, attend classes, and work in a drug-free environment.
- a COMMUNITY VOLUNTEER who would like to rouse your organization to take action against drug abuse, but you don't know where to begin.
- a PROBATION OFFICER, SOCIAL WORKER, or HEALTH CARE PROFESSIONAL who would like your co-workers to respond more helpfully and knowledgeably when they address adolescent drug issues.
- a TEACHER or COUNSELOR who is caught in a no-win situation because you can't ignore the fact that every day you see kids who are in big trouble with alcohol and other drugs, but you can't persuade parents or school administrators to support your efforts to do something about it.
- an ALCOHOL/DRUG ABUSE PROFESSIONAL who wants programs on chemical abuse to be set up in your community's schools, but you can't convince school staff members and administrators to take your ideas seriously.
- a SCHOOL ADMINISTRATOR who has a budget that barely covers the expense of an extra bottle of glue, let alone

the expense of a new program, but you find the need to do something about student drug problems weighing heavily on your mind.
- a SCHOOL DISTRICT SUPERINTENDENT who would like to confront the problem of adolescent chemical abuse, but you fear that if you so much as admit that the problem exists, you'll catch nothing but flak from the media, parents, and other school district superintendents.
- a CONCERNED PERSON who is frustrated because the drug programs in your community reach too few young people, catch up to them too late, focus on illegal drugs but ignore alcohol, work at cross-purposes, or try to operate in isolation.

In other words, *Alliance for Change* is for *anyone* who wants to help young people refrain from drug use during their teen years and make healthy, wise decisions about alcohol and other drugs during adulthood.

Whoever you are, you probably have seen enough to know that many young people in your community are molding their lives around the delusions and distortions created by the use and abuse of alcohol and other drugs. Some, the defiant ones, seem beyond love, reason, or threat. Others are pursuing the same disastrous course, but with less flamboyance. You know *all* these kids need help. What can *you* do about them?

You *could* seek them out on the street, in the school parking lot, in the alley behind the videogames arcade. Most of them would laugh at your Lone Ranger routine and leave, but some might stay to talk and listen to you for a while, and if you persisted, your concern might make a difference to a few. Maybe. But how long could you work this hard? How long before you would throw up your hands in despair at the sheer numbers of young people you can't reach, the ones who won't listen, the ones who listen and go in for treatment but somehow end up back on the street using all over again?

The challenges confronting you, a concerned person, are great. The odds seem to be stacked against you. There are just too many kids in trouble and too few adults who share your concern. The odds are no better, however, for any single agency or group of trained professionals in your community. There are just too many kids with too many problems that manifest themselves in too many different ways and in too many different places. The odds are against all of us—unless we work together. This book tells you how to shift the odds in your favor.

Alliance for Change is a blueprint for action, *your* action. It shows you how to start where you are—with what you know about the problems in your community, with your feelings about them, and with those people who share your concern. You can call on outside experts for information and advice, you can bring in movie and television stars to talk about drug abuse, and you can read this book, but the truth is, no celebrity or consultant can ever know as much about your community as you do. In the end, you and the other concerned persons in your community must make the necessary changes.

You will be taking the first steps in forming an "alliance for change" by reading this book and sharing its information with others in your community. You can be well on your way to successfully mobilizing your community as you implement the following guidelines for action:

- Assemble a task force of concerned persons who will act as agents of change within their own spheres of influence.
- Assess your community's problems and resources.
- Design programs that will meet the needs not only of the young people who are already involved with alcohol or other drugs but also of those who have not yet used any mood-altering chemicals.
- Approach, lobby for, and win the support of key persons in your community.
- Identify and overcome the most common barriers to action.
- Maintain a broad base of community support.

Not everyone who reads this book will want to become involved in a communitywide enterprise of such broad scope. I've presented this comprehensive approach, however, so that each reader can see the big picture and decide how he or she wants to fit into it. For instance, some counselors will choose not to participate at all in program development but will continue to work in direct service with young people while supporting and utilizing the new services developed by others. Similarly, some parents will decide not to become active members of a task force or a parents group but will support mobilization efforts when a county board or a school board holds hearings on the subject. As you read, then, try to see how your skills, interests, and position in the community best match the recommendations made. Be an active reader even if you do not intend to participate in every phase or aspect of this communitywide effort.

The information in this book has been distilled from years of experience—my own and that of the many hardworking people I have met during the past ten years—in working with schools and communities across the country. You can use it to attain the goals that your group or community has identified as the most important and the most urgent.

The flexible guidelines provided here are already working—

- in rural communities such as Glendive, Montana, where people come from hundreds of miles around to learn how to set up effective programs in their own areas;
- in sprawling suburban areas such as the Greater Cleveland area, where 64 school districts have joined forces with one another and with scores of community groups to tailor specific programs for their kids; and
- in dozens of other communities, large and small, where people have begun with little more than their own anger, frustration, concern, and stubborn hope.

These guidelines for action will work in any community where people have the patience to plan carefully and the determination to persist until they achieve their goals.

* * * * * * * *

This book is divided into two parts. Part One describes the futile approaches used by adults to "solve" the adolescent drug problem, barriers to action, and the process of community mobilization to set up a school-based early-intervention program. Part Two recounts how people in Ohio and Montana have joined forces to make changes in their communities and offers the personal accounts of individuals who have worked hard to change their own systems.

Part One

CHAPTER ONE
A Time of Reaction

Generations of adults have used the euphemism "the facts of life" to refer, somewhat glibly, to the inevitable realities of growing up: learning about sex, morality, and individuality; acquiring various techniques for surviving in the world; making decisions and accepting the consequences of those decisions. Most of us, as adults, think we know all about the facts of life. After all, we've all been down that road. Today, however, there is a new fact of life, a new inevitable reality. Most of us don't understand this reality well enough to think clearly about it, let alone guide and advise our children about it. This reality is drugs.

It is a fact of life today that few, if any, adolescents can avoid being exposed to drugs—alcohol, marijuana, tranquilizers, stimulants, hallucinogens, to name a few. For a few kids, drug use may retain some of the "expand your mind and learn new truths" aura that accompanied the rise of adolescent drug use in the 1960s. For some, it may be a way to avoid stress and problems. For others, it may be a way to gain prestige among their peers or to feel grown-up, sexy, or confident. And some kids may use drugs for all these reasons. There is no single motivation for drug use and no typical user profile.

Unlike their parents and grandparents, the young people of today do not consider drug use to be particularly outrageous. In today's world, the use and abuse of alcohol and other drugs are almost the status quo. According to one government survey on alcohol and other drugs,[1] 56% of the high school students in this country try alcohol before they reach tenth grade and 60% try marijuana before they graduate. And we are talking about kids here, for the average age of first experimentation is now 13 or 14.[2] Results of a 1981 poll published by the *Weekly Reader*[3] showed that 25% of all fourth graders felt "some" to "a lot" of peer pressure to try alcohol and other drugs.

Clearly, alcohol and other drugs are so accessible that *all* kids have a decision to make. For some, it's whether or not to begin experimenting. For the others, it's whether or not to continue using. Without some guidance from the adults who care about them, will they be able to make sound decisions? Too many will not. Many will be hurt and many will not survive the consequences of their decisions.

We all know something about what can happen to those kids who do use drugs. We've heard stories about our friends' kids or the kid down the street. We've heard that 31% of all 10th, 11th, and 12th graders are problem drinkers;[4] that the leading cause of death for 15- to 24-year-olds is alcohol-related highway accidents;[5] that the 28 million children presently living with alcoholic parents are three times more likely to become chemically dependent than the children of nonalcoholic parents.[6]

Stories and statistics abound, and they all point to the same conclusion: Adolescent drug use is a big issue today. It is a new fact of adolescent life. Yet by our ongoing ignorance, denial, confusion, and failure to take effective action, we allow our young people to make their decisions about drugs in a vacuum. Learning the facts, understanding the issues, deciding on an appropriate plan of action, and adopting a strong, well-organized, and coherent approach to adolescent drug use are among the greatest challenges facing adults today.

DRAMATIC BUT FUTILE APPROACHES

In the years since the use of alcohol and other drugs by adolescents became an urgent and demanding problem, adults have reacted to it in many different ways. We've argued about its causes and have discussed ad infinitum where to put the blame: on families, churches, police, schools, television, societal

To make wise decisions about alcohol and other drugs, adolescents need guidance from adults.

alienation, or the perpetual threat of nuclear war. We've outraced one another to be the first to set up a program, some program, any program that could solve the problem once and for all. We've put drug sellers behind bars; we've kicked drug users out of school; we've pushed through laws mandating drug education in the schools. A few of these measures have been somewhat productive and others, less so. Yet all of them have been "reactions," and they have *not* solved the problem.

So our initial optimism has degenerated into pessimism. We've let the drug problem become a political football—something to use against an incumbent politician or an issue behind which a sheriff or police chief can rally the community, whether or not he or she has anything new to offer. Our approaches have swung from one extreme to the other.

If we look at the approaches that have achieved a certain popularity in past years, we find that they underestimated both the nature and the scope of the problem. Some had an immediate impact on the community, but their long-term effects ran counter to any effort to help kids and their families. Others could have had merit if the community had not focused all its energy and hope on them and excluded other ideas. Without exception, all of them were just partial solutions, reactions instead of actions.

How have we reacted to drug use by young people in the past? What works and what doesn't? It makes sense that if we want to improve on a design, we must first examine and understand the original design. If we don't learn from our own and others' mistakes, we are likely to "reinvent square wheels." And if they wouldn't roll for others, they probably won't roll for us, either. Some highly touted approaches that have fallen short of expectations are paraphernalia crackdowns, law enforcement efforts to make drugs inaccessible by "getting the pusher," undercover police operations to ferret out drug users in the schools, use of police dogs to sniff out drugs, and celebrity testimonials about the harmful effects of alcohol and other drugs.

Crackdowns on paraphernalia sellers

Many communities have tried to stop adolescent drug use and abuse by making the sale of drug paraphernalia illegal and cracking down on those who sell it. There is nothing wrong with this approach when it is part of a broader effort to rid the community of drug and alcohol abuse. More often than not, however, it represents a reaction to being caught unawares by a drug subculture that seems alarmingly alien. Something similar to the following scenario has probably occurred in every community in this country:

> Quizzical Mom confronts her 14-year-old daughter who has come in the front door and is on her way out the back, late again for her dance class.
> "Wait! What is this thing, Susan? I found it in with your gym clothes today."
> Susan's eyes widen at first sight of the object in Mom's hand—a pipe for smoking hashish—but she glances quickly at the clock and says, "Oh. That. It's a . . . glitzmarph."
> "A WHAT?" Mom asks. "What is it for?"

To improve programs, we must learn from past mistakes. Square wheels won't roll.

"It's for a sort of game. Everybody has 'em now, Mom."
"Where in the world did you get it?"
"Oh, you get 'em at the dime store, record stores, everywhere. Actually, that one isn't mine," says Susan in her best offhanded manner. "Can I have it now? I should give it back to the guy who loaned me it."
" 'Loaned it to me,' you mean. All right. Sure is an awful-smelling thing, though," says Mom, wrinkling her nose in distaste.

Kids who use drugs can fool a surprising number of adults for a while, but they can't fool all adults forever. The gadget may be called a glitzmarph, but the game is "getting high." When we adults find out that we've had the wool pulled over our eyes, we react with fear and outrage to quell what we see as an invasion by foreign elements. While our reaction is understandable, our solution is as ineffective as our definition of the problem is oversimplified.

Does the legal sale of drug paraphernalia sanction illegal drug use? This question has absorbed much anger, frustration, and energy in many communities, but it remains a red herring. In other words, it distracts us from recognizing that making alcohol, other drugs, and paraphernalia illegal for kids has not stopped them from using. Unfortunately, if kids want to use drugs, they will find a way to obtain or improvise the necessary gadgets (cigarette papers and pipes can't be declared illegal). If all else fails, they can usually buy in neighboring communities whatever they can't get in their own community.

In communities where concerned adults have lobbied, won votes, changed laws, and finally succeeded in pushing all paraphernalia sellers out of town, young people have continued to buy, use, and abuse drugs. The crackdown on paraphernalia sellers has not changed kids' attitudes about getting high.

Apprehension of "pushers"

One misconception has severely impaired our effectiveness in dealing with adolescent drug use and abuse: If we could stop the pusher, we could eliminate the problem. This idea has some validity, perhaps, at the state, national, and international law enforcement level. In our schools, however, the pusher

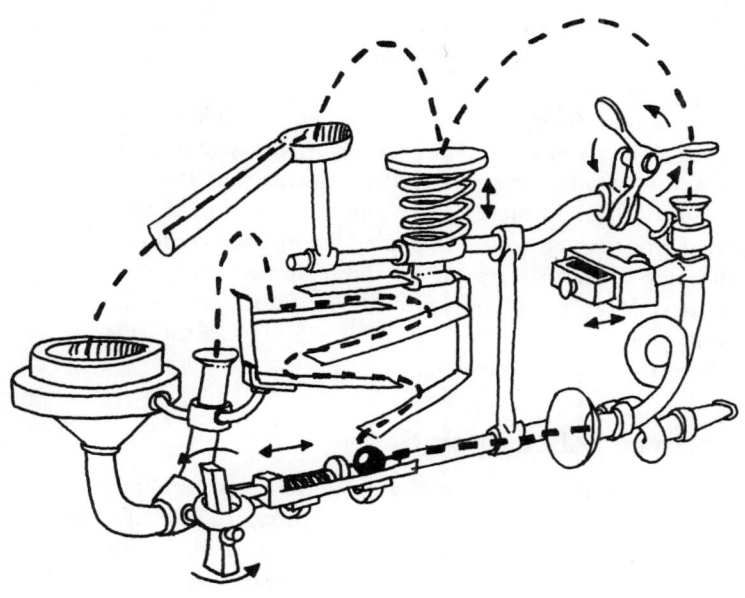

Outlawing paraphernalia won't stop kids who want to use drugs. They'll find a way to obtain or improvise the necessary gadgets.

becomes a shimmering, elusive mirage when we try to pin him or her down. The following brings this point home:

> In a survey[7] of sixth graders in a suburban Minnesota school district, students were asked, "Which ways do you most often use to get alcohol (beer, booze, etc.)?" A startling 25% indicated that they most often got their alcohol from parents, a finding that caused the school to embark immediately on an education project to teach parents about the effects of alcohol on young people. Since alcohol was by far the most commonly used and abused drug in the community, it would seem that most of the "pushers" in the community were parents.

Where do kids get the illegal drugs they use? From one another, from their brothers and sisters, from older kids who get them from one another. They get alcohol not only from these same sources but also, as revealed in the survey just cited, from their parents—with or without their permission—and from unobservant or complacent liquor store owners or clerks. All of these people and others are part of the drug-sharing and drug-selling culture in which we live.

Look closely. From your own experience, can you identify a pusher, someone who single-handedly is luring kids into trouble with drugs? Is there even a single source for all the drugs that are causing trouble for the kids in your community? Probably not. Drugs are readily available almost everywhere in this country. More than likely you'll never find a real pusher; you'll only find kids who need just as much help as the kids with whom they share their drugs.

Undercover police operations

One approach that has received local and national publicity in recent years is the undercover police operation. To identify and apprehend drug sellers and users, a detective provided with a false identity and outfitted with a teen-style wardrobe poses as a student at school. A variation on this approach is the "bounty" program, in which students themselves inform the police about their drug-using peers and are rewarded with money.

Such operations do indeed result in numerous arrests and much publicity. Their supporters contend that arrests, punishment, and publicity continue to make the consequences of illegal drug use clear and obvious. They presume that fear of the consequences is enough to keep students from using drugs.

They presume incorrectly, however. While undercover and bounty operations may have a preventive effect on marginal drug users, they aren't likely to have any impact on kids who are already harmfully involved with drugs. The following example clearly points out the shortcomings inherent in this approach:

> An undercover police operation was tried several years ago in a town of 26,000 near Boston. Since then, a psychologist in the local school system has reported[8] that he and many of the students with whom he has talked are opposed to such methods, not so much on principle but because the actual outcome did not seem beneficial.

Want to stop the "pusher"? Kids get alcohol and other drugs from friends, siblings, and even their parents.

"I can see what they were trying to accomplish," said the psychologist. "I can applaud that much. But what they did was useless. Even the level-headed students, those you might call conservative, became disillusioned with the police and the other institutions that were involved. The kids who got caught were kicked out of school for a year, and I'm not so sure that they were ever reinstated. Most of those caught were not really the heavy users or sellers. The heavy users and pushers just got a big chuckle out of it. It was poorly handled by all sides, including the media. They just sensationalized what could be sensationalized. I don't see that anything constructive came out of it for the kids, for the schools, or for anybody else. Drug use continued unabated in the school."

Before you agree to an undercover police operation in your community, then, closely examine its likely short-term and long-term effects by answering the following questions:

- Who will be apprehended—heavy users or casual users and experimenters?
- Will the kids whose drug of choice is alcohol believe that liquor is "safe" because no one is paying any attention to it?
- Will the children who are arrested, kicked out of school, and put on probation be given any help? Does such an approach include counseling and treatment?
- Will future transfer students face suspicion and hostility from other students who fear that these new students may not be who they say they are? Will the student who returns from treatment be suspected of being an undercover "narc"?
- What values do young people learn when they grow up in a community where people covertly report on one another, not out of loving concern but for money?
- Does an undercover police operation do anything at all to encourage individuals to speak up out of concern for their own, their spouse's, or a friend's possible problem with alcohol or other drugs?
- Will students, their parents, the school staff, and the community at large be any wiser about drug use and abuse as a result of an undercover police operation?

All these questions—and the answers—are very important. When detection, apprehension, and punishment are a community's primary focus, the answer to the last two questions is a resounding NO. If anything, such an approach adds to the alienation and mistrust already pervasive in the community.

In light of these adverse effects, ask yourself one more question: Do you really need undercover detectives to identify which students are using drugs? Probably not. Just ask teachers and other school staff members; they no doubt already know. If they won't act on what they know, they more than likely think school policies are excessively punitive, know policies are erratically enforced or support services are lacking, or fear reprisals and lawsuits from parents.

Some people espouse a wide range of approaches to the youth drug problem. In addition to favoring some types of drug education and early-intervention programs, they believe in undercover police operations because, they say, "It is necessary to do all that we can to stop the drug problem." Well, *the catch is that these efforts are not cumulative. The fear and distrust generated and the actual harm done to students by undercover operations are antithetical to the kind of atmosphere needed to develop truly effective early-intervention programs.* You cannot have it both ways. If your school district has undercover police officers posing as students, early-intervention and prevention efforts will be greatly impeded.

Use of police dogs

Another dramatic approach is to bring in police dogs specially trained to sniff out stashes of marijuana, hashish, and other illegal aromatic substances. With this approach, you do rid the school of *some* of the chemicals that students are using—at least for a while—and your actions do proclaim that drugs will not be tolerated. Unfortunately, dogs can't detect capsules or tablets. What's more, they ignore alcohol, even though it is the most widely abused drug in our high schools and is illegal when used by minors.

For any serious and comprehensive antidrug program to work, the penalties for drug use must be made clear and enforced consistently. Even so, detection and punishment alone will not solve the problem. Some kids will decide not to risk experimenting with drugs; others will merely stash and use their drugs elsewhere. By bringing in the dogs we might change some of the outward customs of drug use, but we won't reach the students who most need our help.

The "show-biz" approach

The "show-biz" approach involves hiring a celebrity who has kicked a drug habit to warn kids about drug abuse. It has definite appeal because it takes only a few hours, thus minimizing disruption of the school schedule, but what does it accomplish?

Well, for a week or two after the celebrity's appearance, teachers may recognize paraphernalia and glassy eyes and a few kids will ask for help or more information. For the most

Police dogs can sniff out illegal aromatic substances, but detection and punishment alone won't help kids.

part, however, it will be business as usual in the hallways, restrooms, and parking lots. For every student who now fears the risks involved in drug use, another has been made aware of, and is intrigued by, all the exotic paraphernalia, drugs, and mood-altering effects. And the media get a good story, which takes the heat off the school in the aftermath of a serious drug incident.

If an effective early-intervention program is already in operation, the appearance of a celebrity can increase interest in and referrals to the program. On the whole, however, the show-biz approach simply provides a temporary balm to soothe inflamed media and exasperated parents who are relieved that the school is finally taking responsibility for a very frightening problem. Its long-term effects on the community and drug use are minimal.

No matter how effective at the outset, anything done just once or twice a year to stop the use of alcohol and other drugs by adolescents is doomed to fail. In the early 1970s, show-biz and other one-shot approaches were undertaken with naive optimism, but they were a first step. Today, knowing what we do about kids, drugs, programs, and what works and what doesn't, using a one-shot approach to solve this multifaceted problem is next to being irresponsible. It is a small step above doing nothing, one that will have to be taken repeatedly, because without genuine support the changes that do occur will quickly fade away.

There are no panaceas. There are no easy solutions.

THE PENDULUM EFFECT

American editor and writer H. L. Mencken said it: "For every complicated problem there is a simple solution . . . and it's usually wrong." Faced with kids' perplexingly determined behavior and distressingly blasé attitudes about drugs, we adults often cling to "simple solutions," including paraphernalia crackdowns, apprehension of pushers, undercover police operations, bounty programs, and celebrity testimonials. Too bad that none of them are effective.

What happens, then, when these "solutions" fail? All too often the net result is the feeling that nothing more can be done. Such resignation is only temporary, however, because eventually something must be done.

Imagine the high school in your community or any high school in any community during a period of reaction. The following scenario would not be too far off the mark:

> For years teachers and other staff members ignore students who are smoking marijuana in the school parking lot. Then one day the community decides to crack down, spending thousands of dollars on an undercover police operation that makes examples of just a few of the many students who use and sell drugs. As many as possible are arrested. For the most part, however, drug use by students remains a big problem. Finally, the community admits that little has been changed for the better. When the program becomes too expensive or unpopular because of lawsuits, countersuits, and parental fury, it is dumped.
>
> The problem is forgotten—until half the football team gets busted for drinking or using other drugs. Blame is tossed around like a hot potato—until someone decides that drug education is the key. A while later some kids are hurt or killed in an alcohol-related highway accident, and the community responds, "Look! Education doesn't work, either!" Sporadic attempts at education are alternated with harsh crackdowns and then give way to resignation. The pendulum swings back and forth, often with political factors accelerating its speed.

From one generation to the next, from community to community, from family to family, or—at the very worst—from situation to situation, the pendulum of our reactions swings from extreme to extreme. We not only are giving mixed messages to our kids but also are wasting our energy and resources, spinning our wheels, going nowhere.

Adults' role in the problem

Most adults contribute to adolescent drug abuse unwittingly, in spite of their good intentions. Examples abound in every profession: counselors who prefer to be trusted confidants rather than confronters; teachers who refuse to see what's in front of their faces, partly because they truly are oblivious; superintendents who back away from admitting that drugs are a problem for fear of political consequences affecting their

Our reactions to adolescent chemical use swing like a pendulum from one generation to the next.

careers; psychologists who ignore drug use and ascribe all adolescent problems to underlying personal and family difficulties; police officers who are adamant about arresting teenagers who use marijuana but continue to tolerate teenage beer parties; clergy who are so openly hostile to drug use by teenagers that they scare off anyone who wants help for a drug problem; and physicians who too readily prescribe tranquilizers, antidepressants, and diet pills. Then there are the parents who think nothing of helping their 16-year-old celebrate his or her birthday by providing beer for all the kids at the party.

Clearly, to effect a change in kids' perceptions and use of alcohol and other drugs, we have to reach adults first. Only by educating parents and professionals will it be possible for us to achieve the balance needed to overcome the problem.

THE NEED FOR BALANCE

We adults must strive valiantly to strike a balance between being rigidly restrictive and being permissive. We must try to find a functional middle ground between harsh punishment and perfunctory reprimands for young people who violate laws or school regulations on drug use.

Parents don't want to give their children the impression that they expect them to drink. Not at all. But they also say, "If you do drink, please don't drive. Call us if you need a ride home." Is there a danger here of giving a mixed message? Sure there is. Is there a possibility that this may save someone from being paralyzed or killed in a drunken-driving accident? Sure there is. Similarly, when a counselor in a drug awareness program allows a young person who admits to using drugs to stay in a support group, is there a possibility that the counselor is enabling him or her to continue using? Definitely. If this young person is treated in a punitive manner—immediately referred for disciplinary action—is it possible that other members of the support group will not be open about their own drug use? It is not just possible; it is inevitable.

If you think I'm making a pitch for "responsible" use of alcohol and other drugs by adolescents, you're wrong, dead wrong. On the contrary, I firmly believe that we can start immediately to expect absolutely no drug use by kids at school or at home. We can also turn back the tide to the point where we can realistically expect young people not to drink until they reach the age at which drinking is no longer illegal or until they are mature enough to make responsible decisions about alcohol use . . . whichever comes last.

We *can* reach this happy state of affairs, but it requires balance. On every level of intervention for drug and alcohol problems, we need a balanced approach. For adolescents, nonuse must become the norm and the use of chemicals the exception. If we want to tell our kids to call us when they are too drunk to drive, fine. But then we have to sit down with them the next morning, when they are sober, and discuss the problem and our expectations in meticulous detail. If a counselor, parent, or school administrator allows a student who has had a "slip" to stay in an aftercare support group, that

A Time of Reaction

Individually and collectively, we need a balanced approach to adolescent drug use.

adult had better know the difference between effective intervention counseling and simple enabling. If he or she doesn't, members of the aftercare group can be sidetracked onto a disastrous course of dealing with nothing but slips instead of working on recovery.

A balanced approach involves more than the careful consideration of each problem that arises. For a balanced approach to be truly effective, it must be adopted by the community. It makes sense that we can be more successful in keeping our own children away from alcohol and other drugs if the parents of our children's peers are also working to achieve this goal. It stands to reason that we can be more successful in preventing kids from driving while drunk if we are also willing to confront our adult friends who drive while under the influence.

If the pendulum effect is inevitable in social history, perhaps we can start to strike a truly effective balance by making each successive swing of the pendulum a little less severe, a little less extreme. We can begin to expect our young people to refrain from using any chemical, but we can't try to pummel them into submission. We have to work with them, to make our expectations clear, and to be consistent and fair in making rules and in meting out consequences for the breaking of those rules.

Unless we adopt a balanced approach to the problem of adolescent drug use, we will continue to act like the fabled blind men who each touched a different part of the elephant and then argued about whether it was more like a snake, a wall, a whip, or a tree trunk. We will not begin to have a real impact on adolescent drug use until we combine forces and stop being willfully blind to the nature of the beast.

* * * * * * * *

Drug and alcohol use *is* a fact of adolescent life in this country. We have seen that lopsided reactions and narrowly focused programs have been and will continue to be counterproductive and short-lived. In the next chapter, we'll begin to look at some basic strategies for successful intervention against the use and abuse of alcohol and other drugs by adolescents.

CHAPTER TWO

Changing the Game Plan

To help young people beat the odds in the fight against drug and alcohol problems, we have to change our game plan. In the past we have reacted like videogame players, using bursts of determination to fire off single volleys in as many directions as possible. True, we did have some impact using this approach; we did help some young people, and some of us changed our own and others' attitudes about adolescent drug use. We just didn't have enough impact to get ahead of the game. Now we have to pull back and think again, think ahead. If we are to develop coherent, balanced, long-range, effective programs, we need a different approach—the calculated approach of a patient chess player. In our game, strategy counts more than fast reaction time.

Any strategies we devise rest, implicitly or explicitly, on our assumptions about drugs and drug-related problems. While hundreds of assumptions affect our attitudes and actions in various ways, five basic issues cry out for attention; these issues come up again and again when communities begin to mobilize. I'll begin with a consideration of five basic assumptions that I feel are crucial to effective communitywide action. Then I'll discuss three general strategies for community mobilization against adolescent drug use: networking, community intervention, and the intervention-to-prevention approach. These strategies serve as the underpinnings of the components of early-intervention programming, which will be described in Chapter Three.

THE NEED FOR AGREEMENT

Whether it's a chess game, a government, or a drug intervention program, if the people involved don't use the same terms and agree on some basic assumptions, they are unlikely ever to focus on common goals. In my experience, all of us committed to helping kids who have drug problems must agree on five basic assumptions. If we don't, confusion will seriously hamper, if not stalemate, our efforts. These assumptions are as follows:

- Alcohol, in all its forms, is a drug.
- A range of drug use problems necessitates a comparable range of intervention techniques.
- Problems related to drug use are not the sole criterion for intervention. Drug use alone, regardless of the presence or absence of observable problems, often warrants intervention.

In our game plan, strategy counts more than fast reaction time.

- Drug use can be the priority for intervention even if it is not the primary problem but the result of another problem in the user's life.
- There is no need to compromise on drug use; adults can expect teenagers not to use drugs, especially on school grounds and at home.

The drug alcohol

The field of adolescent drug treatment and early-intervention programming has seen a proliferation of terms that seem to differ subtly in meaning. We hear about chemicals, drugs, mood-altering agents, psychoactive substances, substance abuse, problem drinking, alcoholism, chemical dependency, and addiction, to name only a few.

With this proliferation of terms has come confusion. When a speaker refers to chemicals, one listener thinks of illegal drugs, such as angel dust and THC. A second infers both illegal drugs and alcohol, while a third is momentarily distracted because he associates the term with sodium nitrate and carbon tetrachloride. Clearly, it is to our benefit to agree on the meaning of some common terms, at least within this context.

Let us agree, then, that for our purposes the terms "drugs," "chemicals," and "mood-altering agents" mean all drugs used for mood-altering or recreational purposes, that is, for their effects on the body, mind, and mood. By this definition, *alcohol is a drug*. It may be a drug traditionally and legally used by adults, but its traditional and legal status doesn't change its nature or its effects. Ethyl alcohol is a potent chemical that depresses the central nervous system and, in some users, has a brief stimulating effect. When taken in strong enough doses, it can kill. When abused over time, it can wreak devastation on the physical, social, psychological, emotional, and spiritual life of the abuser.

A range of problems, a range of intervention techniques

There are those who argue that for adolescents, it is pointless to try to separate use from abuse, that all use is abuse. While it

"Your drug of choice, madam?" Alcohol may be a substance traditionally and legally used by adults, but it is still a drug.

is, in fact, futile to try to determine the specific point at which use becomes abuse, it is important to realize that there are many reasons for young people's involvement with chemicals, many different degrees of severity of drug problems, and a variety of appropriate actions that can be taken to tackle a drug problem. For instance, while many young drug users can benefit from an intensive primary treatment program, there are those who do not need such services. Similarly, those kids who can benefit from immediate and forceful disciplinary action stand in contrast to those for whom disciplinary actions make no difference at all. If we adults are not willing to make a distinction between the person who merely uses drugs occasionally and the person who is physically and psychologically addicted to drugs, or between the person who has a single drink at a party and the person who gets drunk and then drives like a madman with friends in the car, then there is no hope of our developing an effective communitywide response to drug problems.

Problems related to use not sole criterion for intervention

It has become fashionable in some circles to voice the following bromide: "Schools have a right to intervene on a student's drug use only when that student is manifesting some problem related to that use. If a student is using responsibly, then the schools have no right to intervene."

However sensible this may sound, it is a seriously flawed approach to adolescent drug use. Take the case of a college-bound straight-A senior who is caught drinking at a party near the end of the school year. If this were the only evidence of drug use, we would probably agree that it would be a waste of resources to do a full-fledged assessment to determine whether or not he has a drug problem. But what about a 10-year-old who has a couple of beers two or three times a week, is still doing as well as ever in school, and is not causing any trouble at home? Aren't there a multitude of reasons why we wouldn't want to allow her to continue drinking?

We know that the earlier a person starts using drugs, the more likely he or she is to have chronic problems with chemicals later in life. We know that the physical growth and development of a 10-year-old can be harmfully affected or inhibited by drug use. What's more, a 10-year-old has playing to do, discoveries to make, and pleasures to experience. Using drugs is a passive way to generate joy; it involves no thought, imagination, or skill. Drugs are an alternative to self-generated joy. Youngsters must learn how to make themselves happy; if they rely on drugs in this process, they inhibit their capacity to find joy in many aspects of adult life.

Another important point in this argument is that *it is not possible to tell when problems actually begin*. A young person may start having trouble with comprehension long before it shows up clearly on a written test or in any marked behavioral deficit. When we talk about problems related to use, we are really talking about *observable* problems. Many problems progress to a serious stage before they are detectable.

Given that most, if not all, of us would agree that drug use, even with no apparent adverse effects, is not appropriate for a 10-year-old, we then have to decide at what age seemingly problem-free drug use ceases to be an issue. At age 11? At 12? At 14? At 16? The tremendous differences in physical and emotional maturity among young people further complicate the issue.

Consider the case of a 16-year-old student who uses marijuana and alcohol four times a week. He has an IQ of 120 and a considerable competence in mathematics. Should the fact that he can do algebra problems as well as or better than any of his classmates even when he is under the influence of drugs deter his parents or teachers from taking steps to stop his drug use? Hardly. Parents and educators have an investment in

The idea of "responsible" use for adolescents is seriously flawed; at what age or size does a young person become "responsible"?

helping a young person attain not just minimum standards but maximum potential. If a student can solve basic mathematics problems while under the influence of chemicals (some can, most can't), then she or he needs more stimulation and should be taking calculus or advanced computer courses. Also, performance is not the only measure of academic success. If possible, we want to help young people find joy in learning without that experience being dampened by drug use.

Another point in this argument is that although the presence of use-related problems is *one* indicator of future drug problems, their absence tells us little. Young people who use drugs but manifest no apparent problems may be ensnared in a more quiet, insidious process that will eventually lead to chemical dependency. Often, personal style or family background dictates whether drug users do or don't get into obvious trouble. More than likely the kids who tend to act out or play the role of "family scapegoat" will be rowdy or destructive when using drugs. In contrast, the "family hero" may start using drugs heavily at age 15 or 16 and not manifest any problems until he has become addicted to alcohol by age 18 or 19. The quiet, shy, ingratiating young man liked by everyone may be far ahead of his more disruptive peers in terms of having a serious, long-term problem with drugs.

I wish to emphasize here that use-related problems cannot be considered the *sole* criterion for intervention. Certainly, the degree of seriousness of a young person's problems will affect how we handle an intervention, how much we will invest in it, and what types of risks we are willing to take to ensure its success. Drug use alone, however, is a very legitimate reason to intervene, not only for parents but for educators as well.

Priority for action versus primary problem

Many professionals and researchers disagree about the exact nature of drug dependency and addiction in young people. Some contend that regardless of other problems in their lives, young people can be chemically dependent and addicted in the same ways that adults can. Others argue that since kids' primary problems are likely to be rooted in family problems, sexuality, or issues of personal identity, these underlying issues must be addressed before the "symptom" of drug abuse can be altered.

"Priority for action" and "primary problem" are two different concepts. It could be said of an epileptic who has violent seizures that her broken bones are secondary to her primary problem of epilepsy. However, no one would keep her from receiving emergency treatment for a broken arm because she is scheduled to attend her regular session of group counseling for epileptics or to see her physician to have her response to antiseizure medication checked. The priority for action in this case would be to have the broken bone set.

Similarly, an adolescent's drug use may well be secondary to being physically and/or sexually abused. Although drug use may be only one of several psychological and behavioral problems calling for intensive treatment, it can be the priority for action. If his or her heavy use of marijuana cannot be stopped, it will interfere with any treatment program undertaken to deal with the trauma caused by the physical and/or sexual abuse. (If a child is still being abused or is still in danger of being abused by a parent or anyone else, the priority for action is, of course, to remove him or her from the home, regardless of the drug problems he or she or any other family member may have.)

No need to compromise

Kids have a right to grow up in an environment free of the intense pressure to use drugs that pervades many of our schools and communities today. Adults have a right to expect that young people will not indulge in casual drug use. Of course, there will always be some young people who experiment with drugs, but they can become the exception rather than the rule. A drug-free environment can become a reality if we don't compromise. If we start compromising on drug use, we may not find it easy to stop. The more compromises we make, the harder it becomes for us to imagine a line of resistance, let alone draw it firmly and maintain it staunchly.

Some of us may find it more difficult to hold the line on alcohol use than on the use of marijuana and other drugs. We may feel that since we ourselves use alcohol, we would be out of line telling young people not to use it. There is a certain lack of assertiveness among those of us who are confused about our own position on alcohol. We may be attempting to justify our own use by saying that alcohol is not a drug and is intrinsically less dangerous than illegal drugs. Once alcohol is labeled a drug, however, we have to take a different stand, perhaps a more threatening one. We have to say that although we do use alcohol, we realize that no one should drink without first considering the possible consequences, that a certain degree of maturity is needed before a person can use alcohol safely, and that the use of any mood-altering chemical must be avoided until a person has successfully tackled the many basic developmental tasks of adolescence. We also have to admit to ourselves and others that we are taking risks when we use alcohol and that the assessment of those risks demands a measure of maturity and experience not possessed by adolescents.

Let me reiterate. Nonuse of all mood-altering chemicals on the part of young people is our goal, one on which we need not compromise. We do have to recognize, however, that we are a long way from making this goal a reality. Let's not become unduly discouraged, though. We can accomplish more, with less, sooner than we imagine.

GENERAL STRATEGIES FOR COMMUNITY MOBILIZATION

As I've already stated, the three general strategies for community mobilization against adolescent drug use are networking, community intervention, and the intervention-to-prevention approach. Before we explore these strategies in detail, however, let's take a close look at the challenges presented by young drug users. The following examples bring them into focus and provide a clear picture of the need for these strategies:

> *Marti.* What could you do to help someone like 14-year-old Marti? Her family just moved to town and she's not doing well in school. Her parents don't know if she's having a hard

time because she's staying out late and hanging around with a tougher, more worldly group of friends than before or because she's experiencing the difficulties normally involved in adjusting to a new environment. They feel guilty about having taken her away from her old friends. They also feel angry and worried. After a few stormy scenes at home, Marti admits to drinking and using other drugs with her friends but swears she'll run away if her parents try to stop her. Her parents don't know anyone in town to whom they can turn for help.

Tom. How could you change things for someone like Tom? His older brothers and sisters were all regarded as troublemakers by the teachers at school, and Tom seems bent on following the same path. He usually comes to school late looking sloppy and tired. Since he has a reputation for backing up his words with his fists, no one challenges him when he brags about how much beer he and his father put away the night before. Tom has managed to get through school so far by doing the bare minimum of work. When the rumor reaches the teachers lounge that he's on probation for some crime—no one is quite sure what he did—the consensus there is that he'll never graduate.

Eric. What could you do for a teenager like Eric who is afraid that a family member is in big trouble with drugs? Eric knows that his cousin Bill has been buying and selling drugs; he has even been along when Bill has made pickups. In the beginning, Bill justified his actions by saying he needed to make extra money so that he could buy some new clothes, a present for his girlfriend, and in a couple years, a car. Lately, however, all the money seems to go for buying drugs for himself. Bill now seems desperate, but he won't talk to Eric about the crazy way things have changed. Since he's gone along with Bill this far, Eric is afraid to tell anyone. He thinks that if he talks, he'll probably just get them both into more trouble than they're in already.

Cheryl. And how would you help someone like shy, nervous Cheryl? Long suspected by teachers of using drugs, Cheryl was finally caught when she dropped her purse on the school stairs and a bottle of her mother's tranquilizers fell out. Cheryl often comes to school looking disheveled and tired, and once she had a black eye. Talking about her parents, she says, "Yeah, we fight a lot, but we're really a close family." Cheryl's drug use is an obvious problem. No one knows, however, if it is her major problem, and no one seems brave enough to find out.

These examples are abbreviated and simplified, but they do illustrate the kinds of problems that young people face and the kinds of decisions both kids and adults must make about alcohol and drug use. Clearly, no single solution will help all these young people. Should we tell Marti's parents that responsible use is OK as long as she just drinks and doesn't use other drugs? Must we sit back and watch Tom become a hardened criminal before we take any action on his behalf? Would we tell Eric to give his cousin's name to the police even though his community has no court-based program to help drug users? Could we just "tough-love" Cheryl into straightening out and taking full responsibility for all the problems in her life?

No matter how many other factors we have to juggle as we start establishing programs—staffing, funding, writing policies

Shy, withdrawn students like Cheryl may be in greater danger than their rowdy, defiant peers.

and procedures, and handling publicity, to name a few—we have to keep a broad perspective of what kids need. All our efforts should be tailored to doing whatever must be done in our communities to help the young people in need. So let's turn now to the three general strategies for any community mobilization effort against adolescent drug use.

Networking

Whatever the immediate goal, whether it is to persuade the schools to set up support groups or to convince local businesses to support public drug education programs, those people in the community who have contact with and are responsible for the welfare of young people must communicate and cooperate with one another if their efforts are to be successful. This interaction is often called "networking." Those communities that are making some headway against adolescent drug use do *not* relegate this problem to the province of any single agency, institution, or program. Recognizing that kids with drug problems affect almost every aspect of community life, they have developed a network of concerned adults from all walks of life to help these kids.

To be viable, a network should include alcohol/drug abuse experts or counselors. Many others, however—professional service providers, parents, concerned citizens—will play roles congruent with their personal responsibilities, concerns, and interests. Let's look at how the four examples described at the beginning of this chapter could be handled in communities where an adequate range of individuals and agencies make up a viable network:

> *Marti.* In Marti's case, her parents could call a school counselor, teacher, or administrator who is working in an early-intervention program within the school and is trained to deal with issues related to drug problems. In addition to providing personal advice or counseling, this school staff member could help Marti's parents connect with a parents group. These parents could support the stand that Marti's parents must take with their daughter and help the two of them develop some guidelines regarding such matters as curfew, school attendance, and drug use. If the parents of some of Marti's friends belonged to this parents group, they

could combine forces to establish appropriate norms for the entire peer group that would preclude late-night partying, casual curfew violations, and other behavioral problems.

Tom. If Tom's school offered early-intervention services, he could be referred quickly for an in-school preliminary assessment because his teachers would have been trained to report problems regarding physical appearance and academic performance to an early-intervention program counselor. Instead of a rumor about Tom's involvement with the juvenile justice system passing through the teachers lounge, all relevant information could be gathered and assessed so that the counselor would have some concrete data to discuss with Tom and his parents. If the information gathered indicated that Tom had a serious problem with chemicals, the counselor could advise an in-depth assessment by an agency in the community and, ultimately, referral to an inpatient or outpatient primary treatment center for chemical dependency. The treatment program would place a strong emphasis on family counseling.

Eric. Trust is the biggest issue for Eric. If he could see that the services offered by the school and the community definitely helped people like his cousin Bill and if he could be certain that the adults involved would not be punitive, he would be much more likely to take action. Also, if it were clear to Eric that he could talk to a specific person in his school, in his church, or in his family about his concerns for Bill, he would know how to take that first, crucial step toward helping his cousin.

Cheryl. Cheryl and others like her tax the range of community services available to young people. Most states require counselors to report suspected parental neglect and physical abuse to a welfare or family services department. These agencies must be adequately staffed with adults who are sensitive to and capable of addressing the neglect and abuse as well as the obvious drug problem. Since many behaviors related to drug use overlap those related to parental neglect and abuse—absenteeism, truancy, poor grades, depression—all community services must be alert to the possibility of multiple problems in kids who use drugs. If, after appropriate consideration of issues related to parental neglect and abuse, Cheryl were referred to inpatient treatment, the staff of the facility would be made aware of the family problems and could then develop a treatment plan that reflects the fact that Cheryl is not the exclusive source of all the personal problems she is experiencing. Responsibility for working through these problems would be shared by all family members.

As you can see, a range of services and a high degree of communication among the people offering those services are necessary. The concept of networking expands further when individuals who are working with drug problems on a case-by-case basis begin to realize the need for changing entire systems and developing new programs to deal with the many drug-related problems in their communities. The following examples illustrate this point:

> A *probation officer* becomes frustrated when she realizes how deeply her young clients' drug problems are rooted in their parents' problems with alcohol. She decides to join a task force working on a school-based early-intervention program and successfully pushes to have that program include groups for children of alcoholics. After she has been trained, she serves as a volunteer facilitator of one of these school-based groups.
>
> A *county family services worker* obtains permission from the local high school principal to set up abstinence support groups and insight groups* after school hours. Through these groups, not only does he become more effective with his own clients by working with their peers but he also reaches students he would never have seen at a time when their drug problems are still in an early stage. The success of these groups generates support, first from the parents and then from the community as a whole, for a school-based program. After helping to train teachers and community volunteers to lead the groups, he withdraws from the school-based program to work in other areas.

As these examples clearly show, the problems presented by young people can pressure adults into developing a community network for dealing with drug problems. Ultimately, effective networking leads to the creation of a wide range of services in a variety of systems. The success of this general strategy lays the groundwork for obtaining the broad base of support needed for community mobilization, the topic to be addressed in Chapter

---

*Both the concept and the term "insight group" originated at Community Intervention, Inc. In these groups, students caught using or in possession of drugs are helped to examine their own use. These groups often serve as an alternative to suspension, expulsion, or court fines. Participation is part of a preliminary assessment process and may lead to a further referral for counseling or formal assessment.

Four. The primary benefit of networking, however, is that by combining their efforts, all the people in all the systems can reach more young people than any of them could working in isolation. No one has to go it alone!

Community intervention

In trying to garner support from any system's members, more than likely you will come face to face with what appears to be a solid wall of denial and inertia. Some will say they're too busy to talk to you at all. Others will seem bored by what you have to say. Still others will react as though you had insulted them merely by bringing up the dread subject of drug abuse. In fact, many will react in much the same way that families coping with alcoholism do: They will *deny* that the problem exists, minimize it greatly, or display total resignation to it. You won't have to delve too deeply, however, before you discover that the denial and inertia are an icy veneer concealing hot feelings of anger, fear, guilt, and blame. The second strategy, then, is intervention to scrape off the veneer of denial and inertia and begin a process of positive change.

A strong parallel can be drawn between families and communities affected by unacknowledged drug problems. Let's look briefly at a family's denial of the problem:

> Dad is afraid of what his bosses and co-workers will think if it comes out that his eldest son, Dan, is a drug addict. Mom denies the situation to hide her guilt about having failed (or so she believes) to be a good mother. Dan's brothers and sisters are furious because the whole family has already turned itself inside out coping with and adjusting to the problems Dan has caused; if they admit now that he's got a drug problem, he'll get even more attention. So, rather than face their fear, anger, guilt, and anxiety about changing the status quo, all of them are blaming someone else—the school, Dan's friend next door, even "Uncle Joe, who has always been a bad influence." They've banded together to maintain a conspiracy of silence; they've decided to live with their pain rather than let anyone add to it by attempting to "cure" Dan's problem.

Community members react in much the same way as these family members. They deny that young people are in trouble.

To help solve the wide range of drug problems that confronts us, we need the support of people from many systems and many walks of life.

They hide their own confusion, guilt, anger, and pain because they refuse to acknowledge the problem or because they believe nothing can be done to improve the situation. The problem of alcoholism and addiction is shrouded by intense shame, as though its very existence points to a moral weakness that might infect everyone who recognizes it. The attitude that it's safer and less painful to play blind, deaf, and mute complicates the problem immensely. Even if you never work directly with kids and families, be aware that you will encounter denial in other persons and other systems. Thus, the general strategy of community intervention parallels family intervention and consists of these important steps:

- *Acknowledge personal concern.* One person becomes urgently concerned about the problem and decides that something must be done about it.
- *Find other concerned persons.* This person contacts other concerned persons and the group meets to discuss the problem in the community.
- *Seek education.* Each group member learns whatever he or she can about the problem and about specific ways of dealing with it.
- *Pool the data.* Group members seek information and pool the data and their insights about how the problem has affected specific individuals and the rest of the community. In other words, they break the conspiracy of silence.
- *Present the data.* Members of the group present this information to key persons in the community—firmly but without judgment, anger, or blame. Caring and concern must be expressed.
- *Offer a plan of action.* Members of the group provide these key persons with a concrete plan of action that offers real hope for immediate change.
- *Prepare alternatives.* If no action is taken by those who have the power to make changes, the group moves ahead with other plans.

The general strategy of community intervention provides a basic outline for approaching people on any level in any system. We *can* remove the veneer of denial and inertia that is part of the drug problem by being informed, firm, and able to offer hope. We can mobilize a given system to take action by intervening on that system and reaching its key members—those who can help the most—with the hope that they can do something tangible and positive about a situation they consider hopeless. Most adults really *do* want to help kids.

The intervention-to-prevention approach

The value of prevention has been a topic of much discussion in recent years. Some communities have become discouraged because drug education programs are not taught well or regularly or are not taken seriously enough to make much difference. As a result, they are giving up on prevention and settling for short-term actions geared toward dealing with kids who are in serious trouble now. Other communities have seen such a high relapse rate among young people who've gone

Most adults really DO want to help kids.

through treatment that they are giving up on those already involved with drugs and investing all their hopes and energies in long-term programs set up in the elementary grades.

Waiting to intervene on kids until they are in the most serious stages of drug-induced self-destruction is a little like parking the ambulance at the bottom of the cliff and waiting for someone to jump. However, ignoring the kids who are jumping off the cliff while steering the younger ones away from the edge isn't a viable alternative, either. Students in grade school, even though steeped in prevention information from grade one, will still be prey to the pressure to use drugs in the seventh, eighth, and ninth grades. Instead of prevention efforts raising the age of first drug use into the higher grade levels, the example of rampant drug use in junior and senior high will continue to override prevention efforts and steadily lower the age of first use.

Clearly, then, the optimum arrangement is to combine strong prevention efforts with strong early-intervention efforts. Many, if not most, communities that have been successful in their struggle against adolescent drug use have done this very thing. However, if a community doesn't have the resources to implement early-intervention and prevention programs simultaneously, the best approach is to intervene first with the kids most in need of help. The first successes in intervention can provide the momentum needed to achieve success in the second effort, prevention.

* * * * * * * *

By agreeing on the five basic assumptions about drugs and drug use and adopting the three general strategies for community mobilization, we can build a solid foundation for further action. Doing so also prepares us to deal with the "slings and arrows of outrageous fortune" that will inevitably befall our early efforts. In the next chapter, we'll look at the common barriers that confront any action against drug problems. We'll also consider a few tools—in the form of basic program components—that we can use to overcome these barriers when they arise and recur in various systems.

CHAPTER THREE

Barriers to Action, Components of Change

Over the past ten years I've traveled to many communities, met with scores of concerned persons, and advised them on how to develop drug and alcohol programs. My work has taken me from small rural townships to large suburbs; from cities with plenty of money to Indian reservations with very little; from progressive, liberal areas to conservative districts where tradition is tradition and no one changes anything without the say-so of those who have the say-so. I've learned much about how individuals and communities work when challenged by drug problems.

During these years I've come to know that for all their diversity, communities in this country are alike in one respect: They resist changes concerning adolescent drug use by erecting barriers to action. Some of these barriers could be called human foibles—"That's just the way people are." Others are clearly part of the denial and delusion system of alcohol and drug abuse. Basically, these barriers are the same in every community and they operate in the same ways: They prevent people first from *seeing* what must be done and then from *doing* what must be done.

In this chapter, we'll face these barriers head-on, see how they block action, and consider what happens if they are not addressed and overcome. I'll also discuss the basic building blocks of early-intervention programs: awareness and education presentations, identification and referral services, continuum of

Barriers to action are inevitable in every community, but they need not mean the end of the road.

counseling and treatment services, and support groups and activities. These program components can help us overcome the inevitable barriers to action.

COMMON BARRIERS

You may recognize some of the following barriers immediately; others you may not. My guess is that you will encounter all of them if you work very long on drug issues. It is essential to recognize these barriers for what they are and to remove or circumvent them. If they are not addressed, sooner or later they will undermine any efforts to make changes.

Delusion, denial, and fear

One comment I hear quite often, especially from those who are just beginning to look at the adolescent drug problem in their community, is: "It's very hard for us here. Too many people have their heads stuck in the sand—they won't even admit that there is a problem."

This never surprises me. Delusion and denial are the main pillars of addiction and the constant companions of all other drug problems. They are, in fact, part of the classic definition of addiction. When faced with a problem involving alcohol or other drugs, few individuals will just up and admit it. That much we can expect. How we deal with delusion and denial, how we remove this barrier, depends on the fear on which it rests. People can be afraid for many reasons:

- Some may be afraid that they'll be blamed if they talk about their friend's or spouse's or child's drug problems. Or they fear that they'll lose their relationship with this person.
- Some may be afraid that if they point a finger at someone else's problem, that person will point at them. Many individuals are not comfortable enough with their own drinking or drug use to comment on anyone else's.
- Kids may fear that if they talk about drug use and abuse in school, their friends will ostracize them. Many young people adhere to an unwritten code that states it's not OK to open up to parents and teachers about drugs.

- Teachers may be afraid that if they talk about drug problems, they'll be asked to get involved. Or they may even fear that they'll be sued because of their accusations.
- Public school administrators may be afraid of political fallout; if they speak up about drug problems, their districts may be labeled "drug havens." Private school administrators may fear losing tuition-paying students.
- Mom may keep secrets from Dad because she's afraid that he'll get angry. Or they both may keep silent because they may be afraid of what the neighbors will think. Or they may be afraid that if they seek help, their son, the star hockey player, will be kicked off the team.
- Everyone may be afraid that by talking openly about drug problems, the consequences will be punitive and damaging instead of helpful.

The primary fear, then, is that talking about the way things are will somehow make matters worse. Rarely is this the case, however; it is *not talking* that exacerbates the problem. To give you an example, I was asked to speak to a group of teachers shortly after one of their colleagues had died of a drug overdose. "We knew she was taking a lot of pills," they told me, "but we were afraid that if we told anyone, she'd be fired. The strike last year caused a lot of bad feelings."

These co-workers did what they thought was the right, protective, and caring thing to do by not speaking up. This teacher may or may not have been fired if they had spoken up but as it turned out, their hiding her problem didn't help her, either.

When we encounter resistance in a school, probation department, family, or any other system that we approach, we can be certain that fear will be at the base of it. Trying to do something about this barrier can be threatening. It often seems safer, at first, just to deny the whole issue. In the long run, however, denying that the problem exists just prolongs the agony.

Delusion and denial must be countered with perseverance, honesty, and open communication. Fear will be a barrier for as long as we live with alcohol and drug problems. How do we deal with our own fear? How do we conceal it? How does fear block our good intentions? If we don't look at fear and hopelessness and strive to counter them with courage and optimism, even the best programs will be sabotaged from within.

Blaming

When denial or minimizing is no longer possible and we finally have to face the fact that alcohol and drug problems exist in our families, schools, and communities, we tend to blame others.

When parents realize that their child is in serious trouble with drugs, they often turn on each other. One says, "If you hadn't been so tough on him all these years . . . ." The other one says, "If you'd stay home once in a while and spend more time with him . . . ." Feeling panic-stricken, helpless, and alienated, they search for someone else, anyone else, to blame for the problem.

When they don't get very far blaming each other, parents can contend that the school is at fault because that's where kids get their drugs. Educators usually snap back with this retort: "Our business is the three Rs. We're supposed to teach your kids, not rear them. That's your responsibility as parents."

As pressures mount within the community, everyone plays the blaming game. Parents criticize educators. Educators blame the police. The police reproach juvenile justice officers. The courts point to mental health care professionals or to the clergy, who point at parents. And everyone blames television, advertising, pharmaceutical companies, the liquor industry, the Mafia, the breakdown of the nuclear family, and "the way life is today." In effect, everyone is saying, "Until the police [or parents or the mental health care system or the Mafia] change their ways and do something, I shouldn't have to do anything. It's not my fault!"

While the adults in the community are caught up in the blaming game, what are the kids doing? They are using and abusing chemicals, of course. The problem will not fade away. In fact, it escalates.

All the blamers are right about one thing: They all play a role in allowing the problem to continue. But the reverse can

As pressures mount within the community, everyone plays the blaming game.

also be true: If they start to work together, they all can help to solve the problem. The anger that accompanies feelings of alienation and helplessness can be rechanneled to fuel constructive efforts, but first people must decide what their own positive roles should be. For example, how can probation officers help young people in trouble with chemicals? What can teachers do? To whom can they refer kids for assessment and help? Can parents groups be helpful? How?

I can't stress enough that the blaming game stops as we learn to acknowledge and accept our part not necessarily in causing drug problems but in allowing them to continue. Positive action starts as we begin to rely on one another for help. No one individual can solve the problem alone and no one agency or institution can, either. The success of this endeavor depends on the combined efforts of a team of dedicated people working in every system in the community.

A narrow perspective

Once the blaming stops and the search for solutions begins, the next barrier to overcome is the narrow perspective held by many adults concerning the problems and the programs needed to solve those problems. For example, when confronted with the finally undeniable fact that young people are using and becoming addicted to drugs, some adults focus solely on the drugs. They want to know about their pharmacological aspects, appearance, physical effects, and street names. They also want to know about all the paraphernalia. They bring in experts to teach them the details, but somehow they fail to find out what they themselves can do about drug use and abuse. Then, when they find a student using one of these drugs or carrying the paraphernalia in her purse, they have the facts but no plan of action. In and of itself, detailed information about drugs will not help anyone.

Other adults indulge in an overwhelming interest in and emphasis on statistics. People stuck on statistics ask such questions as:

- How many young people use marijuana? How often?
- How many kids at what age have tried this or that drug?
- What percentage of kids who start with alcohol or marijuana eventually use and abuse other drugs?
- Who uses which drugs?

Undoubtedly, this statistical information is useful at many stages of the problem-solving process. It can be used to alert the powers that be to the magnitude of the problem. It can be used to bolster persuasive arguments and funding requests. The point is, we have to *use* the information; becoming walking computer printouts helps no one. If a friend's son or daughter is in trouble, knowing how many other kids of the same age in town or in the state or across the nation are in trouble with the same drug won't help. To solve the problem of adolescent alcohol and drug use, we must first look at our own families and then at our neighborhoods, school districts, and communities because these are the places where we can make a difference. Then, if we have energy and time to spare, we can start working on the national level!

Other adults narrow their perspective by limiting their efforts to young people who are acting out. Many young people who are harmfully involved with chemicals defy the law and their parents and teachers, vandalize property, and engage in other destructive activities. While these kids certainly warrant immediate intervention, they constitute just the dramatic tip of the iceberg of problems caused by drug abuse and alcoholism. What about those who don't act out, those whose pain is silent and invisible? For example, the children of alcoholics are often forgotten when drug programs are set up. Yet they are at very high risk for becoming chemically dependent, and the alcohol problems in their homes will eventually affect their own and others' lives.

The abuse of alcohol or other drugs is a process and a problem that manifests itself in many ways and thus necessitates a wide variety of intervention techniques. With a wide perspective we can design and implement the comprehensive approach needed to solve this problem. With a narrow perspective we may win a battle or two but lose the war. So maintain a wide perspective.

Good drugs, bad drugs

The attitude that there are "good" drugs and "bad" drugs is another barrier that limits our chances of success. As I've already indicated, most people in the United States seem to think alcohol is the OK drug. We've grown up with it. It is an accepted part of American life, and so are its effects. How many jokes have you heard about drunkenness? How many comic strips in your daily paper feature a bar setting? How many comedians make a good living imitating drunken behavior?

Our traditional acceptance of alcohol and its effects too often results in myopia. For example, too many coaches in our high schools ignore the athlete who drinks but turn in the athlete caught using another drug. Both students may be in serious trouble, but good-drug myopia prevents one of them from being helped. Given the fact that nearly half of our high school students use alcohol on a weekly basis,[1] a great many adults—not just coaches—must be looking the other way.

A narrow perspective on the problem of adolescent chemical use limits our chances of solving it.

In contrast, many people who grew up during the 1960s, when the drug culture flourished, think marijuana is the OK drug. They disapprove of alcohol but defend their own and others' use of marijuana. They claim that marijuana doesn't produce the same serious and often tragic effects that alcohol does.

Unquestionably, there are many differences among drugs, but in many ways, mood-altering drugs, including alcohol, are more similar than different. The attitude that one drug is bad, the enemy, but another drug is good, the tradition, is very damaging. It prevents us from seeing the harm caused by the abuse of *any* drug.

Good kids, bad kids

"Good" and "bad" are powerful labels, especially when we attach them to young people. As we work to help kids who are using drugs, this "bifocal vision" can undermine our effectiveness.

Who are the good kids? That's easy: They're the ones who never cause trouble. There are others, of course, who stray from the path a little. We have to watch and guide them, but they're still good kids. Who, then, are the bad kids? They're the ones we don't have to tolerate. They've crossed over some fine line and therefore are beyond guidance, beyond help. Teachers, administrators, counselors, probation officers, youth workers, and parents all draw their lines in different places, but few think they have to be responsible for a kid they've branded as bad.

The good and bad labels affect the way we react to kids who use and abuse drugs. It's natural for each of us to respond more favorably to some young people than to others; some just seem to "hook" us more than others do. However, this natural but selective responsiveness sometimes becomes a barrier to effective action. When a bad (or unlikeable) kid creates problems, we send her off to other authorities. When a good (or likeable) kid gets into trouble, we simply cannot (or will not) understand it. "She isn't a bad kid," we think. "There must be a reason why she did what she did." So we call the good kid in for a little talk. Her reasons may sound

Few people think they have an obligation to help kids who have crossed the fine line between "good" and "bad."

implausible, unconvincing, and even downright crazy, but we tend to believe them because they come from a good kid.

This natural human reaction results in one form of what those working in the field of chemical dependency call "enabling." By becoming hooked in another's system of delusion, we enable that person to avoid the consequences of his or her drug use and thus to keep using and stay sick.

To overcome this barrier, we must remain as objective as possible. Remember, a good kid with a drug problem is in as much peril as a bad kid with a drug problem, maybe even more. What's more, neither of them is the enemy; drug use is.

Promises, promises

This barrier often follows on the heels of the "good kids, bad kids" barrier. After we have accepted a good kid's reasons for negative behavior, we make her promise never to act that way again. She knows we believe in her; our rapport seems strong enough that a promise should give us some leverage with her. We think. Unfortunately, since the chances are very good that someone who gets into serious trouble with drugs once will do so again, such promises are broken more often than honored.

Whether or not clinically considered "chemically dependent," a young person whose drug use is out of control probably has a stronger relationship with the drug than with herself, you, or anyone else. This is a central element in the dynamics of drug abuse. Chemicals, after all, alter the user's mood. They make the drug user feel good *every* time they're used, which is more than any of us can do as a friend, parent, teacher, or counselor. How can we hope to win? We can't. By trying to compete with drugs for influence over the user's behavior, we paradoxically create a personal barrier to action.

This personal barrier is our vested interest in making "our" good kid do what we want her to do. Professionals are as prone to raising this barrier as parents and friends. What happens, then, when the good kid breaks her promise, as she most surely will?

"You're off the team!" shouts the coach. "Get out of this school!" shouts the counselor or the principal. "Get out of this house!" shouts the parent. "Get out of my life!" shouts the friend. All of us are outraged that she has broken her promise and betrayed our vested interest in her. We retaliate because the issue now is our hurt feelings rather than her involvement with drugs. Whether this tangled state of affairs results from naiveté or arrogance concerning our own influence, the result is the same: The troubled child doesn't receive the help she needs.

Ain't it a shame?

When we run up against all these barriers, it's not surprising that we crash head-on into another barrier—the attitude "Ain't it a shame?" Sometimes it's voiced like this: "We'd really like to do something about chemical abuse, but there've been so many funding cutbacks in our state this year . . . we just might as well forget it."

Or maybe you've heard this version: "It's a national problem! Even if we started programs here, they wouldn't do any good. Television pushes drugs faster than we can work to stop the problem."

And then there is the mournful refrain: "We've already tried everything and nothing works. The volunteers left. Our funds were cut. We just can't seem to make the parents [or teachers or school board members] do what we want them to do."

This attitude can be powerfully convincing and therefore is one of the most difficult barriers to overcome. Usually those who voice it have detailed information about all the obstacles but use it in a way that cuts off all further thinking and action. In effect, they've concluded, "Ain't it a shame that nothing can be done?"

It's a fact: The problem of adolescent alcohol and drug use is fraught with obstacles. What we need is a realistic appraisal of them, *not* passivity and mournful if-onlys. We must take the obstacles into account and ask the creative question: "How will we overcome them?"

I've devoted considerable space to discussing barriers to action not out of cynicism but out of the knowledge that they must be recognized before they can be overcome. These and other barriers will surface in predictable and unpredictable places. Forewarned is forearmed!

What happens when a "good" kid breaks her promise not to use drugs anymore? We become furious, we retaliate, and she gets no help.

Although these barriers are not insurmountable, they can be powerful impediments to progress. Individually each is problem enough; together they can be constant or recurrent stumbling blocks to change. For instance, when members of a community have finally been convinced that drug use by students is not the school's fault, they may resort to haggling over whether or not alcohol use should be considered part of the drug problem. Six months after the community group starts its work, new members may come on board and the haggling may start all over again.

If we are to overcome these barriers when they arise and to offer consistently effective early-intervention services for drug problems, we must develop solid programs with a clear sense of purpose. These programs may be set up in many types of agencies, institutions, and social service settings, but they all need a sound foundation. The basic building blocks of this foundation are the four components of early-intervention programming.

KEY COMPONENTS OF EFFECTIVE PROGRAMMING

Young people with drug problems live in communities that deny and will continue to deny those problems unless we intervene. Our task in working for change is, therefore, twofold: (1) to change the norms that perpetuate the cycle of drug use, abuse, and dependency and (2) to continue to help those who need immediate assistance. Obviously, this huge undertaking cannot be completed all at once. Yet the young people who need help now can't wait for the whole community to change its ideas about drug use. What we need, then, is community programming that will allow us to work toward short-term and long-term goals simultaneously.

Some communities will be starting from scratch in an area with no programs at all, while others will have a head start because of a great variety of available resources. Wherever you start, assess your community's problems and potential in terms of the availability of awareness and education presentations, identification and referral services, continuum of counseling and treatment services, and support groups and activities.

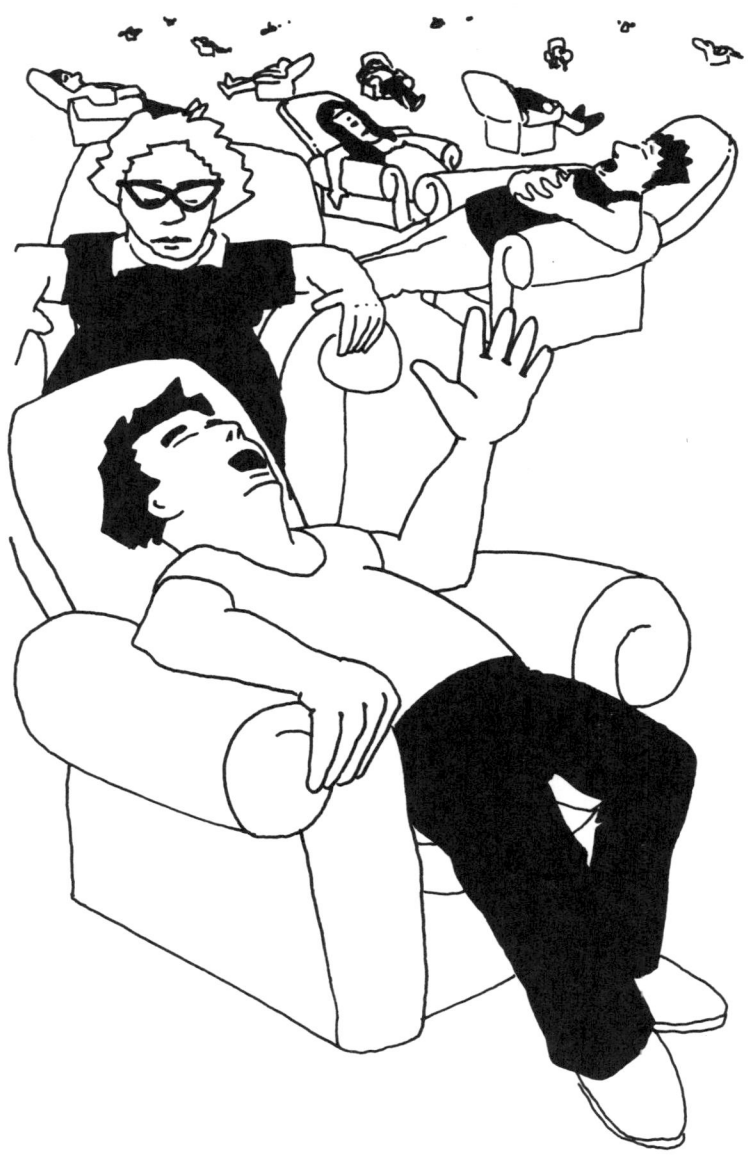

"Ain't it a shame that nothing can be done around here?"

Awareness and education

Many people in your community may know very little about the general problems of drug use and abuse and the specific support resources available. An initial step, then, is to target specific populations that most need to be made aware of the problems—school personnel, parents, social service professionals, and young people. They can be saved much worry and confusion if they know how to recognize potential problems at an early stage and where to seek help once they have identified them. They may also become active participants in a community mobilization effort if they are educated about the serious problems facing the community at present and are given some direction as to how to improve the situation.

Identification and referral

Kids with problems must be identified, assessed, and referred to appropriate support resources for help. The process of identification goes beyond watching for obvious signs of drug use and intoxication. Decreases in academic performance and/or increases in behavioral problems at home and in school must also be noted. One function of a school-based early-intervention program, for instance, is to help teachers focus on students' behaviors. If routine student-teacher interactions do not provide answers as to why changes in academic performance have occurred, teachers can then refer students to staff members of the early-intervention program for preliminary assessment.

Schools are the single best place in which to base services for identifying young people whose drug or other personal problems are interfering with their lives. School-based preliminary assessment services can determine whether drug or other personal problems are, in fact, associated with a student's behavior. The school-based assessment is called "preliminary" to differentiate it from the "in-depth" assessment provided by professional service providers in the community. The preliminary assessment involves seeking answers to very broad questions, the most important of which is, Do school problems indicate in some way the possibility of regular drug use? The exact nature of the student's drug or other personal problems need not be determined by in-school services.

Schools are also the best place in which to set up two types of groups that are very important to the early-intervention process: (1) insight groups, in which students in trouble because of drug use are made aware of the nature and extent of their drug problem and the steps they should take to stop using, and (2) concerned persons groups, in which children of alcoholics and children concerned about a friend's or a sibling's drug use are made aware of how they have been affected by the drug problems of others and are assisted in deciding what they can do to help themselves.

Like the schools, court systems can also play a significant role in identifying and referring for help those young offenders who have drug problems.

Key program components are awareness/education, identification/referral, counseling/treatment, and support groups/activities.

Counseling and treatment

Some drug problems, usually those that occur in the earliest stages of experimental use, vanish as soon as they are identified and appropriate disciplinary actions are taken. A student caught in the parking lot the first or second time she tries drinking in order to be accepted by her peers may stop using alcohol when reprimanded in accordance with routine school procedures.

Other problems, however, cannot be solved so readily. A student with an abusive parent and a three-year drug habit needs more help than a school can offer. To stop using, this young person may need primary inpatient or outpatient treatment followed by long-term family therapy through an outpatient mental health center.

The important point here is that once early-intervention programs begin to identify young people with drug-related problems, services for dealing not only with drug use but also with the gamut of issues that frequently are associated with it must be available. Here, described in brief fashion, are a number of services needed to address the adolescent drug problem effectively. This continuum of care should be available to the community; all the services do not have to be geographically located within the community, and all of them need not be operational before early-intervention programming can begin.

Outside assessment services. Although a school staff member can perform preliminary assessments to determine whether or not problems can be dealt with in the school setting, communities must have a thorough, unbiased assessment service separate from the school. By "unbiased" I mean that the service does not favor one treatment program or one treatment modality over another and does not presume that drug use is the source of all of a young person's problems. Anyone who performs such in-depth assessments must be thoroughly trained in issues related to adolescent development and be particularly sensitive to the possibility that a young drug user may very well be the victim of physical and/or sexual abuse.

Parents groups and networks. Intervention into early experimentation with alcohol and other drugs has been effected by parents working together to establish norms for their children's behavior and consequences for violations of family rules related to drug use, curfews, school attendance, and other issues. Any community can avail itself of this excellent early-intervention method at a low cost. Professional service providers and educators can play important roles in helping parents form groups and networks in their schools and communities.

Outpatient family-oriented services. Family counseling and individual counseling for every family member coupled with appropriate educational services related to drug problems are often sufficient to help a young person who is not yet heavily dependent on chemicals. Professionals competent in dealing with severely disrupted families should handle the most difficult referrals generated by a school-based early-intervention program or a court-based early-intervention program.

Primary chemical dependency treatment centers: outpatient and inpatient. Primary treatment programs designed specifically for young people who have become dependent on chemicals form an important link in an adequate continuum of care. These intensive outpatient or inpatient programs involve four to eight weeks of group and individual counseling.

Long-term residential treatment programs. These programs are for young people who have severe drug problems coupled with serious family or emotional problems. The treatment milieu involves intensive group and individual counseling along with highly structured daily schedules.

Aftercare support services. Based in treatment facilities or specialized community agencies, these services continue the therapeutic recovery program initiated during treatment. Of varying duration and intensity, they are tailored to the personal needs of the adolescents who participate. Services include group work, social activities, individual counseling sessions, and specialized therapy to deal with such issues as incest, sexuality, and grief. Like those young people who have not been through inpatient treatment but want to abstain from using alcohol and other drugs, all adolescents in aftercare programs can benefit from attending Alcoholics Anonymous, Al-Anon, or other self-help group meetings.

Halfway houses. For the older adolescent or young adult whose family situation is so disruptive as to preclude his or her returning to that environment or whose drug problem is so severe as to make it unlikely that he or she can stay off drugs on his or her own, living in a halfway house is a viable alternative. Halfway houses are similar to long-term treatment centers in that they provide a supportive environment and some counseling services for people working toward the shared goals of abstinence from drug use and personal growth. However, halfway-house residents still go to school or work and have more freedom than those living in a highly structured treatment environment.

This is just a bare-bones overview of the types of counseling and treatment services that should be available to the community. Training the staff members of all the agencies serving young people to be sensitive to and competent in dealing with drug-related issues greatly enhances the community's ability to respond appropriately in many different situations. Such staff training proves invaluable even in agencies where the major focus is not drug-related issues.

Support groups and activities

After young people have completed an intensive therapeutic experience or decided on their own that their drug use is harmful and that they wish to refrain from using drugs, they still have many obstacles to overcome. The same pressures that contributed to their drug use continue to exist in their schools, on their jobs, and even in their homes. They need continuing support if they are to abstain from drug use.

Early-intervention programs in schools throughout the country have contributed greatly to the success of treatment and aftercare programs by offering support groups and other activities to young people who have completed treatment. These alcohol and drug abstinence support activities are critical to the success of any early-intervention or primary treatment program.

Support groups and activities in schools differ from the therapeutic aftercare services offered by primary treatment centers and other agencies. School-based support programs do not attempt to continue the basic treatment process; rather, they help young people integrate the changes made as a result of treatment or their own initiative into their daily lives at school and at home.

Incorporation of key program components into various systems

One or more of the four key components of effective early-intervention programming can be incorporated into the services provided by a variety of institutions and agencies, and a wide range of individuals can play important roles in their implementation. Let's take a brief look at how various systems in the community can make use of these components.

Families. Family members can, of course, participate in *awareness and education* presentations as presenters and as audience members. Often, the parents of young people who have completed treatment become extremely active in awareness and education efforts. Based not only on their own experience but also on what their own children and others in the treatment center told them, they are very knowledgeable about the extent of drug use in the community. Also, parents working in volunteer groups can publish newsletters, handbooks, and pamphlets about the drug problem and the intervention programs being developed in the schools and elsewhere.

In regard to *identification and referral,* parents who are aware of the behavioral patterns related to drug use are best prepared to observe and identify them in their own children. They can also be prepared to suggest appropriate action when other parents ask them about how to deal with an adolescent drug user. Parents can do this on a family-to-family basis or through a parents group.

For the young person who has decided to refrain from using alcohol and other drugs, a supportive family environment is all-important. Providing *support* is not always easy. Often, parents must exert considerable effort to change their ways if, in the past, they have contributed in some fashion to their children's tendency to use drugs. In many instances, the changes asked of parents are just as hard to make as those asked of their children. If parents are to help their children refrain from using, they have to become involved in the treatment process and aftercare programs.

In sum, parents are the foundation of the early-intervention process. They can help immensely by being ready, willing, and able to assist their own children and to assist other parents whose children are starting to use chemicals.

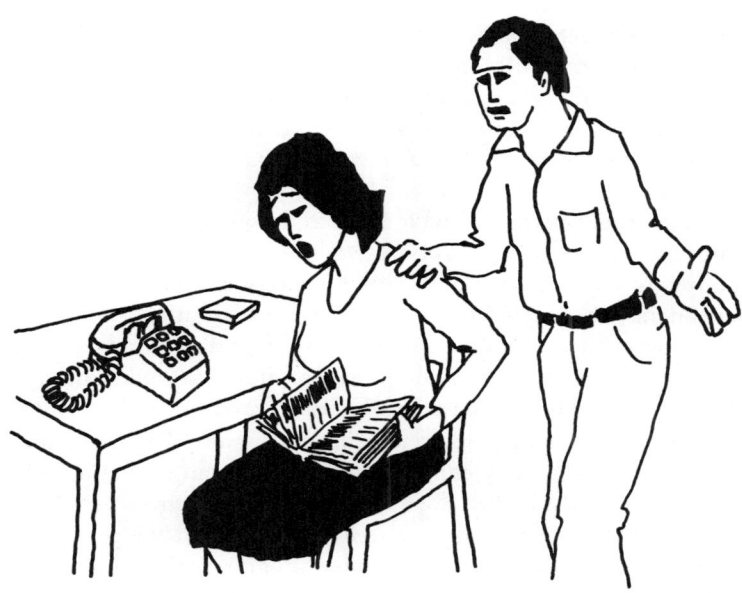

Through community education programs, people can learn how to recognize potential drug problems and where to find help.

Schools. As we'll see later, school personnel have a unique opportunity to help solve the drug problem because they work regularly with virtually all the young people in the community and have direct access to parents as well. The school population is not a select group of young people who have come to the attention of authorities because of their negative behavior or some other distinguishing characteristic. The *awareness and education* presentations offered by schools reach a wide variety of families ranging from those in which there are no drug problems to those in which drug problems are very serious. The schools' awareness and education messages stand an excellent chance of reaching some students *before* their problems become so serious as to warrant treatment as well as those students who are at or near a point of crisis and need help.

School-based *identification and referral* services are also available to virtually all the young people in the community. Within the confines of the school setting, changes in academic performance, negative behavior, and acute intoxication are likely to be observed by numerous adults who deal with students on a daily basis. Their observations can be organized and presented in a manner that will motivate the parents and the young person to seek assistance and change harmful behavior.

While school personnel have little to do with in-depth counseling and treatment services, they can act as resources for counselors working in mental health centers or chemical dependency treatment centers. If, with proper authorization, school personnel provide concrete data about a student's school-related problems, a counselor can put that information to good use during *assessment and treatment planning*.

Because schools are the arenas in which many drug-related interactions occur, they can play a critical role in providing *support groups and activities*. A supportive school environment is invaluable to students who are struggling to resist the pressures to resume drug use and work positive programs of recovery.

Juvenile justice agencies. Juvenile justice agencies can offer *awareness and education* presentations to every client who comes through their doors. This client population is clearly at high

Schools have a unique opportunity to help solve the adolescent drug problem.

risk for having drug problems. Even if there is no apparent evidence of a drug problem in some cases, each client and his or her family can benefit from learning about the problems of drug and alcohol abuse and about available services, should they be needed in the future.

More important than the awareness and education function in juvenile justice agencies is the more direct, action-oriented function of *identification and referral*. Court personnel should be actively involved in screening *every* client for a possible drug problem. Since many of the clients will have dropped out of school, a court-based identification and referral program is a vital addition to any communitywide early-intervention effort.

Juvenile justice agencies also play an important role in providing *support*. Whether they have completed treatment or decided on their own to stop using chemicals, many clients must meet regularly with a probation officer. If probation officers are sensitive to adolescents and their problems and aware of the extreme pressures adolescents face with regard to drug use, they can be of great support to their young clients. The probation department need not provide a formal program but can simply become another voice in the community supporting young people who are not using alcohol or other drugs.

Law enforcement agencies. Law enforcement personnel, particularly school liaison officers, can contribute much to *awareness and education* efforts. Their experiences with the relationship between drug use and crime and their knowledge of laws related to alcohol and drug use are invaluable. Furthermore, when police officers are sensitized to problems of alcohol and drug use and are aware of community support services, they can sometimes perform *identification and referral* functions by helping to direct young people in trouble to the appropriate social service agency.

Mental health centers and other social service agencies. Like the courts, mental health centers and other social service agencies work with a select group of individuals usually at a time of crisis. Such centers and agencies can certainly offer *awareness and education* literature and presentations to alert all of their clients to the problems associated with alcohol and drug use. They can also be actively involved in outreach efforts to educate not only their clients but also the community as a whole about alcohol and drug problems and available services.

Identification, assessment, and referral are very important functions for mental health centers that employ multidisciplinary teams of professionals trained to assess adolescent drug use and the relationship of this problem to other issues. They can do in-depth assessments, whereas schools and courts can only perform preliminary assessments that do not intrude too deeply into personal issues. If its staff members are sufficiently sophisticated in the assessment process, the center or agency can offer its comprehensive assessment services to schools, courts, and other systems in the community.

Mental health centers can also offer appropriate individual, group, and family *counseling* services; they can even develop their own outpatient *treatment* programs for chemical dependency. Social service agencies can make abstinence *support* services available to young people who have completed treatment and to those who are attempting to refrain from drug use on their own.

Medical care settings. Physicians who have served families on a long-term basis are uniquely equipped to do *awareness and education* work with their patients. They can talk with their patients and keep their waiting rooms well stocked with appropriate literature.

Family physicians can also play an important role in *identification and referral*. Over the course of the physician-patient relationship, the physician can verify changes in the health and character of an adolescent patient. Given the high level of trust betweeen physicians and their patients, an adolescent patient's family may well hear a physician's concerns before those of a school official, a police officer, or even a family member. In addition, emergency department staff members who are trained to handle problems related to drug abuse—including but not limited to overdosing—can be key contributors to the identification and referral of young drug users.

Hospitals can, of course, contribute greatly to the continuum of care by providing *inpatient treatment* for young people who have become dependent on chemicals. Knowledgeable staff members in these facilities can give presentations to raise the community's *awareness* of drug problems.

Churches. Churches as institutions and the clergy as individuals can serve as *awareness and education* resources for those who are concerned about their own or others' problems with alcohol or other drugs. By openly discussing adolescent and adult drug use, the clergy can show the members of their congregations that they are willing to listen and help. In addition, if the clergy are able to direct people in distress to various services in the community, they can facilitate the *identification and referral* process.

Spiritual *counseling* can also be an extremely valuable

contribution that the clergy can offer to individuals who are attempting to live without chemicals. Spiritual beliefs and growth are crucial to personal programs of recovery. While this can be true for anyone, whether or not he or she has been affected by professional or self-help services, it is particularly true for many of the people who are dedicated to the programs of Alcoholics Anonymous and/or Al-Anon. Clergy who are familiar with the spiritual aspects of the Alcoholics Anonymous and Al-Anon programs can serve as important links in the continuum of care and support.

Churches can provide *support* by offering the use of their facilities for meetings of self-help groups such as Alcoholics Anonymous and for social and recreational activities for young people who want to have fun without using alcohol or other drugs.

As you can see, all the systems that I've just described have a natural strength for implementing one, two, or three of the four key components of effective early-intervention programs. Very few systems can do it all, however. Also, each system is only as good as the other systems with which it must work. It does little good for the schools and courts to develop excellent identification and referral programs if there is no competent, comprehensive assessment service available or if counseling and treatment services in the area are not up to par. Similarly, hospitals that open an inpatient primary treatment unit for chemical dependency cannot provide effective programs if appropriate clients are not referred to them or if the necessary information regarding clients' problems at home and in school are not passed on to the counselors who are responsible for treatment planning. Also, a hospital-based primary treatment program can hardly make any headway if there is no solid support system in the community once clients complete primary treatment.

Just what emphasis a particular system decides to place on a specific aspect of early-intervention programming depends on a variety of factors, including its current strengths, the expertise and training level of its staff, and the availability of other services in the community. For example, if the community lacks a competent, unbiased, thorough assessment service for young people who appear to have a drug problem, an outpatient social service agency should consider developing such a service. It should also take the time to make the existence of the service well known in the community. If several assessment services already exist in the community, then perhaps the agency should decide to offer another type of early-intervention service. Whatever its emphasis, the agency should ensure that its staff members develop some basic skills to help them identify, assess, and refer appropriately any of their current or prospective clients who appear to have a drug problem.

* * * * * * * *

In this and preceding chapters, we've seen the approaches to adolescent drug use and abuse that don't work and considered the basic assumptions, general strategies, and key program components that do. In the next chapter, I'll present a nuts-and-bolts explanation of the step-by-step process of motivating people to take action, the process of community mobilization.

CHAPTER FOUR
Mobilizing for Action

Initiating programs is rarely easy even under the best conditions, but if people in the community don't know where to begin, if they have no plan of action, it can seem impossible. Community mobilization to help young people who have drug problems can begin at the top, with the support of a county board of commissioners or a local school administration, or at the grass-roots level. Tact, timing, and politicking all come into play, and many variables must be juggled simultaneously.

Community mobilization is different in every community because every community has its own dynamics. I recommend starting with an emphasis on school-based early-intervention programs. In some communities, however, the court system proves the most open to change, while the schools adamantly resist it. Actions taken by juvenile court judges and probation officers can spur family social service agencies, child welfare agencies, and mental health centers to change because these systems must respond to the needs identified by the courts. By drawing attention to these needs, this spontaneous coalition can foment public support for other programs in other systems. People will start to ask, "Can't we reach these kids somehow *before* they get into serious trouble with the law? Why isn't there a treatment center in this town? We evidently need one. What can be done to prevent kids from starting to use drugs?" Faced with such broad community support, even the most resistant school administration has to take action eventually.

In other communities, parents are the primary agents of

change. Because parents are the single largest constituency interested in child and adolescent welfare issues, tax-funded agencies and institutions have no choice but to listen to them eventually.

If people in a court system, social service agency, school district, or community do not show the slightest inclination to do anything about the adolescents in their midst who are drinking or using other drugs, it is best to start small. *Target the system that you know best and work with whatever potential exists there.* If you venture outside your immediate area of expertise, more than likely you will expend precious energy just trying to be heard. It is wise, then, for a parent to begin with parents, a teacher to begin with schools, and an accountant to begin with the business sector. Eventually, the impact of diligent work in one system will be felt in other systems as well.

The key word here is "eventually." Mobilization takes time. How much time and exactly how it occurs depend on the community's unique dynamics. While I can't speak to the specifics, I can try to demystify the overall process of setting up programs by sharing, step by step, what others have done.

MOBILIZATION STEP BY STEP

The step-by-step process of mobilizing communities against adolescent alcohol and drug use ranges from forming an interest group of concerned persons to writing a program proposal to winning approval for the program. However logical, this sequence is not carved in stone. Many steps can be transposed or taken simultaneously if the community has the necessary resources. Some steps need not be taken at all if the community already has some understanding of the problem and is ready to take action. Although this sequence can be streamlined to fit the circumstances, care must be taken to lay a sound foundation for future programs to avoid having to backtrack later if crucial support evaporates.

Step one: Form an interest group

The best way to form an interest group is to look for people who, because of a personal or professional investment in drug

Mobilizing for Action 77

The impact of diligent work in one system will be felt in all systems.

issues, may be interested in talking about the problem. Has anyone expressed concern to you about the extensive use of alcohol and other drugs by young people? Has someone come to you with a problem that may have been connected to drug use, even though he or she may not have expressed it in those terms at the time? Have you ever heard parents talk about how hard it is to keep kids away from a known drug hangout or bar? If so, talk with these parents. If you are a school nurse, do you know teachers who are frustrated about the number of students who are absent from school because of chemical use? If so, talk to them. Does an agency or health care facility in the community offer specialized services for alcohol and drug problems? If so, consult with one of the staff members. Don't waste your energy at this point trying to recruit people who should be but are not concerned. The time to fire both barrels of your powers of persuasion has not yet arrived. You are simply inviting people to take part in an open-ended discussion about drug issues.

If you are just beginning to mobilize your system or community, initial meetings of the interest group can be both educational and stimulating. One person's experiences will trigger another's insights. Others' knowledge will validate your own suspicions about the extent of drug use in the community. Together all of you will begin to break the "no-talk rule" that has kept you separate.

Step two: Focus on appropriate goals

How well you begin to mobilize is no more important than why you mobilize. You can take all the right steps, motivate hundreds of people to rally around stopping the sale of drug paraphernalia in the community, hold a huge celebration when the last "headshop" closes its doors, and still not stop one high school student from getting drunk or high. I do not believe that "anything the community wants to do" is an effective approach. If a community mobilization effort does not focus on the goals of providing early-intervention counseling, treatment, support for refraining from drug use, and other long-term services, it eventually languishes and fades away.

As I've already stated, you may use this book as a blueprint for action to achieve the goals of your choice. However, I'd like to point out some goals of community mobilization that I consider crucial:

- Awareness and education programs should be set up to stimulate widespread recognition of problems related to alcohol and other drugs and available support resources.
- Early-intervention programs should be established in the schools, courts, and mental health centers.
- Adolescent treatment facilities should be created if there are none available to the community.
- Community and school norms concerning adolescent drug and alcohol use should be changed to eliminate "free zones" where drug use has been permitted.

Above and beyond the specific goals just listed is the broad goal of community mobilization: stimulation of community support for a variety of integrated programs that provide a wide range of services for dealing with the wide range of problems caused by or related to drug use. By definition, integrated programs do not work at cross-purposes, as happens, for example, when one social service agency ignores adolescent drug use and focuses solely on psychological or family problems, while a second pledges its energies to punishing "criminal behavior," a third insists on total abstinence, and a fourth accepts "limited" or "responsible" drug use as the norm for adolescents. Unfortunately, social service agencies and helping professionals do tend to protect their own turf. However, if each agency in a community steadfastly insists that its approach is the only approach, there is divisiveness, not integration. Although agencies may disagree on many points, they must be convinced to accept the fact that different types and degrees of problems warrant different approaches.

Step three: Convert the interest group into a task force

Once the interest group has reached a consensus about the need for and the focus of action, the next step is to convert the interest group into a task force, which is an interest group that possesses a good share of power, expertise, and influence.

In large measure, the interest group's focus of action determines which individuals should be invited to become task force members. For instance, if you are a staff psychologist at a private hospital and the focus of your interest group is the creation of a drug treatment program, you might seek out the talents of other psychologists, medical personnel, hospital administrators, parents of patients with drug problems (past and present), volunteers from Alcoholics Anonymous and Al-Anon, school counselors, family social service workers, and anyone else whose skills and special insights can enhance your efforts. If you are a teacher and/or a parent and the goal of your interest group is to persuade the schools to take action, you might ask school staff members, other parents, building administrators, the district superintendent, professionals from the community, probation officers, and volunteers from civic action groups to join the task force.

If you find a key administrator who is willing to participate in the task force, you obviously will have gained a significant advantage. Do not be overly concerned, however, if you can't persuade any administrators to be members at this point. The approval of top-level administrators will be imperative later but is unnecessary at this stage of mobilization. For now, seek out people whose credentials and/or contact with kids or key agencies may make them powerful, articulate advocates of change.

Look for interested and concerned parents, the largest single constituency in any community. Many have become forceful supporters of community drug programs during the past few years and should be included in the task force from the very beginning.

Look for volunteers from civic action groups and from fraternal and sororal organizations. They can rouse support—both money and labor—from their organizations.

You might consider inviting a student to join the task force. A young person who has completed treatment can be a persuasive voice attesting to the need for programs. He or she can also lend credibility to any estimate of the number of young people affected by drug abuse. Do not pressure a recovering student, or any other recovering person for that matter, to take part, however; he or she may have enough to do just working on a personal program of recovery.

Regardless of the task force's focus of action, you should try to include helping professionals—medical practitioners, counselors, alcohol/drug abuse personnel, clergy, juvenile justice officers, social service workers, and others. Their insights and expertise will be invaluable in delineating the drug problem in the community, in designing effective programs, and in expanding the network of involved persons and services. The inclusion of professionals from the start also may help to ensure the longevity of the programs. Parents may think the programs are great, businesspeople may support them wholeheartedly, and administrators may approve of them, but if social service professionals are not cooperative, the programs will not be successful in the long run.

Above all, look for concern and commitment in prospective task force members. I've seen some task forces mushroom almost overnight from 5 to 50 members, most of whom have remained members in name only. Ten individuals who are concerned and committed can accomplish more than 50 with clout who have neither the time nor the inclination to work.

Step four: Train task force members

The training of task force members is invaluable because it generates motivation, commitment, and confidence. For example:

> When one task force member from a small Montana town returned from an intensive, weeklong training workshop on adolescent drug problems, his co-workers decided that he had become too enthusiastic to see all the obstacles clearly. They voted down his proposal to raise funds to sponsor a similar workshop for 70 teachers and professionals. As it happened, he missed the meeting at which they rejected his idea. Oblivious of their decision, he proceeded on his own. At the next committee meeting, he reported that he had already raised a substantial portion of the necessary funds from private foundations and local businesses. The workshop was held a few months later.

Because of this man's single-handed efforts, 70 people in his community gained the same insights, motivation, and confidence that he had. They also forged strong connections with one another in their efforts to combat adolescent drug use.

Task force members usually agree about the need for action. Frequently, however, they disagree about the focus of action. Members inevitably possess varying levels of understanding of the adolescent drug problem, and they often have untested and sometimes unfounded beliefs about this issue as well. Furthermore, few task force members appreciate their roles in perpetuating the drug problem or their potential for helping to solve it. Thus, initial meetings of untrained task force members may lack clarity of purpose and direction; even basic cooperation among members may be missing. If no clear plan of action emerges, meetings eventually degenerate into expositions of "pet projects" or interpersonal conflicts and membership can decline rapidly.

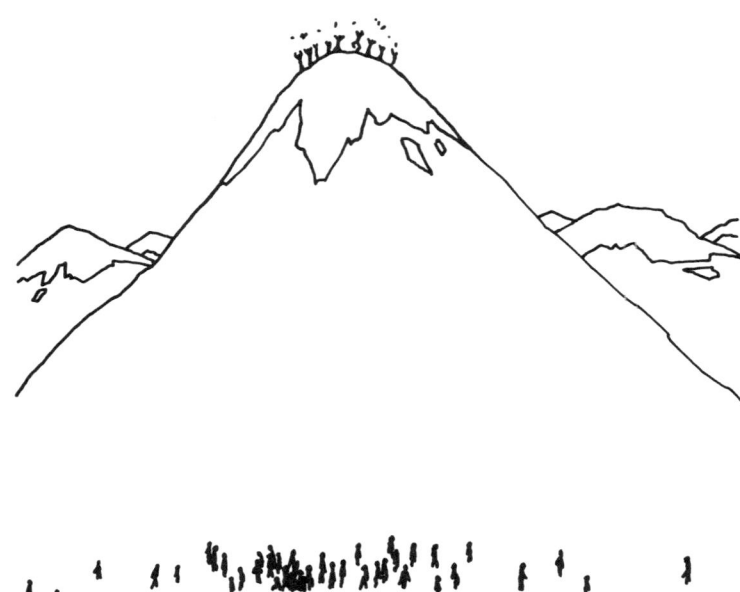

Ten concerned and committed individuals can accomplish more than 50 with clout who have neither the time nor the inclination to work.

The number one antidote to this sorry scenario is training. Effective, professional training can literally transform an assembly of individuals into an informed, skilled, cohesive, energized, task-oriented group focused on community action and change. The major components of effective training are solid, useful, current information; experiential learning techniques; generation of the hope, motivation, and energy needed to complete the tasks that lie ahead; and a clear focus on relevant, action-oriented goals.

Information, experience, energy, goals . . . action.
Effective training for community mobilization against adolescent drug use includes information on such topics as:

- adolescent development and behavior;
- chemical use, abuse, and dependency;
- the effects of drug use and dependency on the family;
- the issues and practical techniques related to the identification and assessment of drug use and related problems;
- referral processes and the appropriate use of community services;
- counseling and treatment for drug-related problems;
- the ways in which family members, friends, professionals, and systems enable young people to use alcohol or other drugs;
- intervention as an individual, system, and community process;
- the history and current status of prevention programming;
- the intervention-to-prevention approach; and
- practical methods for mobilizing communities to make changes in attitudes and behaviors.

Many different formats are used to present this material: lectures, half-day meetings, and information-oriented two- and three-day chemical awareness seminars, to name a few. Of all the possible ways of spurring people to take effective action, the weeklong workshop conducted by experienced alcohol/drug abuse professionals who are solidly grounded in current training techniques is the single best investment of time and money for new task force members. Shorter presentations may

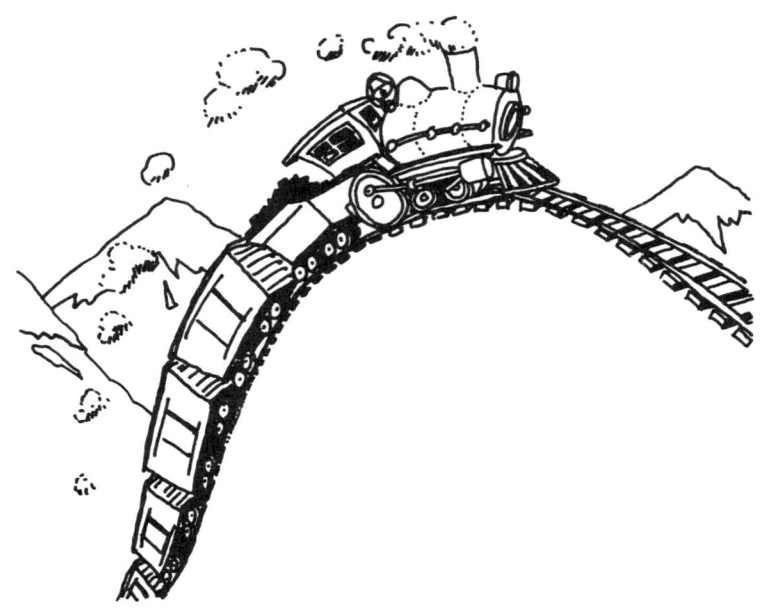

Professional training gives people the information, confidence, and motivation they need to overcome obstacles and achieve their goals.

allow participants to acquire some facts, but only an extended workshop provides them with a full range of learning experiences. Group discussions, role playing, personal encounters with kids who use drugs, challenging of and reflection on the information presented, and simulated planning sessions in which participants set specific action goals for themselves and their communities are essential components of an extended workshop. These shared experiences transform hesitant neophytes into confident, committed, effective agents of change.

An intervention technique.   Effective training is the beginning of the intervention process. The long-term changes needed to solve the adolescent drug problem begin on a personal level for participants when they share their experiences, concerns, and hopes. During training, participants are helped to consider the ways in which they may be enabling the adolescent drug problem to continue and the ways in which their ideas, feelings, and behaviors sometimes make solving the problem difficult or impossible. Small-group discussions help participants develop empathy for those whose lives are disrupted by drug use. Individually and collectively, they begin to deal with the difficulties of mobilizing against drug problems. Unlike training that focuses exclusively on intellectual issues, training that touches participants in such a personal way is more likely to have a long-lasting effect. Personal experiences are shared, perceptions are examined, behaviors are challenged, and feelings are validated. Because such training is individualized, genuine learning occurs.

Many participants also discover that their personal and professional attitudes and behaviors are at odds. During training, participants learn to recognize this conflict and address the many ways in which it keeps them from effectively dealing with the young people they are trying to help.

As workshop participants become aware of their personal and professional identities and accept that their behaviors and attitudes affect their ability to deal with adolescent drug problems, they set the stage for system intervention. Systems change when individuals within systems are healthy, strong, and secure enough to direct such changes. In training, participants learn how the formal and informal rules, styles, leadership, and membership of various systems may be consciously or unconsciously blocking necessary changes. Participants examine their respective systems, analyze the structure, and decide on appropriate approaches to effect changes that will benefit rather than hinder community mobilization.

A profession. To be effective, training must be conducted by a staff of counselors and clinicians who have a wealth of experience in working with individuals plus expertise in community mobilization. The design and implementation of workshops is an art and a science best practiced by professionals who have demonstrated their effectiveness in the field of training.

Many primary treatment centers offer their own training on the subject of adolescent drug and alcohol problems. However, even with the best intentions of providing comprehensive training, treatment centers quite naturally tend to play down the value of assessments, support groups, and family counseling and to focus on their area of expertise, inpatient or outpatient treatment. Such training does not encompass a range of intervention techniques but rather is an outreach program designed to increase the number of appropriate referrals.

An ongoing process. Although I'm emphasizing the need to train task force members very early in the course of community mobilization, I don't mean to imply that training should be limited to this time. As the work of the task force progresses, newcomers who become involved in program development, design, implementation, or operation need their own training experience to become truly invested and fully involved.

I hope I've made it clear that training is the keystone of effective community action. Don't underestimate its value. Spend whatever time and energy it takes to obtain top-quality training. As you consider potential training organizations, remember that the wider the base of trainer expertise, the more likely it is that training will provide the depth and breadth of information and experience that participants need. If an organization can't offer this broad-based expertise, keep looking! You won't regret it.

Step five: Gain formal recognition for the task force

The task force's next step is to approach the governing body of the system on which it is focusing and request that it formally recognize the task force as an ad hoc committee authorized to investigate the adolescent drug problem. Obviously, in a school district, the governing body is the school board. In the juvenile justice system, individual judges or the committee of judges that oversees administrative decisions often holds the real power. In hospitals, this authority rests with the board of directors. In civic action groups, the organizational planning committee can grant this recognition. The important point here is that regardless of the type of system, the task force must identify the real focus of power there and settle for nothing less than direct contact with that person or group.

The main purpose in asking those in power for recognition is to let them know that the task force exists and that it is not investigating the problem behind their backs. If the task force makes it clear that it is *not* asking them to commit themselves to a particular plan of action at this time, they are likely to grant the task force some measure of sanction and authority. If they prove to be especially interested, they may decide to appoint one of their members to the task force.

If, for some reason, the task force cannot gain ad hoc status at this point, it should proceed without it. Once those in power are aware of the task force's existence, they will not be surprised at being approached again, when the task force is ready to present its findings. By being direct about its intentions, the task force can help prevent the spread of damaging rumors.

Step six: Set the task force agenda

Once members of the task force have been trained and the governing body has been approached, the task force can move to the action stage of community mobilization. The key to effective action is the task force agenda. It should include the following items:

- doing a needs assessment;
- writing a program proposal;
- obtaining financial support; and
- making a formal presentation of the program proposal to the governing body.

Admittedly, completing this agenda is a tall order, but it can be done. What's more, the task force need not spend two years or even six months completing it. After all, the proposal is not meant to be the last word on drug problems or their solutions in the community, region, or nation; rather, it should stimulate others to take action. Excellent training in conjunction with effective task force leadership will set the tone and pace of the group. Task force members should be allowed to volunteer for whatever tasks they are able or willing to do. If necessary, however, the task force chairperson should assign tasks and set deadlines.

Step seven: Do a needs assessment

To be able to define and then describe the adolescent drug problem as cogently as possible, the task force must gather relevant data. In other words, the task force must do a needs assessment.

Does "needs assessment" sound like an abstract term relevant only to sociologists and bureaucrats? Don't let the jargon distract you. Human beings have been doing needs assessments since time began. For example, Stone Age hunters who advanced too far north must have discussed what they could do to solve the problems brought on by the extreme cold. Build bigger fires? Wear more clothing? Eat more food? Invent a new kind of shelter? Return to a warmer climate? Whatever they decided to do, it's a sure bet they didn't waste much time doing it. A needs assessment isn't a magnum opus; rather, it is just one important task on an agenda set up to ensure that young people in the community get the help they need.

A needs assessment should address the following questions:

- What is the extent of the drug problem in the community, school district, system, or neighborhood?
- Who is affected by the problem? How are they affected?
- Who is most concerned?
- What support services exist? What services are needed?
- What can be done about the problem now, given the resources and potential of the group, system, or community?

The more thorough the research, the more convincing the findings will be in rousing people to take action. Thoroughness does not necessarily mean quantity, however; emphasize quality. A good rule of thumb is to gauge the extensiveness of the research needed by the amount of resistance expected. If the governing body of the system in question wants the proposed program to be established without delay, the task force should waste no time setting it up. A formal needs

Human beings have been doing needs assessments since time began.

assessment can always be done during the first year of program operation.

A comprehensive needs assessment encompasses the following components:

- a survey of drug use patterns;
- interviews with key concerned persons (for example, parents, health care professionals, school staff members, juvenile justice workers, students, social workers) regarding the extent and nature of the adolescent drug problem;
- a survey of social service agencies offering assessment, intervention, and treatment services to determine when services are available, to whom, and under what conditions;
- a review of current policies and procedures regarding the chemical use of those within or served by such systems as schools, probation departments, and hospitals;
- a review of state and federal laws, regulations, and policy guidelines relevant to drug issues, health and welfare of adolescents, insurance, and other concerns as they affect the system in question.

Even the most limited needs assessment should include some information on the first three items, so I'd like to discuss each of them in detail.

Surveying drug use patterns. There are many ways to estimate the number of young people in a given area who are using or abusing chemicals. The task force may need to do nothing more than collect statistics compiled by other groups. For example, both the National Institute on Drug Abuse (NIDA) and the National Institute on Alcoholism and Alcohol Abuse (NIAAA) can supply an abundance of statistics regarding the various drug use patterns and the effects of drug use on young people. (The address of each organization is listed in Appendix A.) Any state office on alcohol and drug problems can also provide information about drug use patterns in the state or region. If the community already acknowledges the problem, the task force may not need any statistics to gain approval for drug programs. Again, what the task force does to estimate the scope of chemical use and abuse depends on what is needed to convince others to take action.

If statistics for the area served by the task force are lacking, a standardized survey can be a valuable tool for gathering essential data. It can provide a basis by which to compare one area with other areas and the present population with future populations (in order to study changes over time). Appendix B lists some basic questions needed for a standardized survey on adolescent drug and alcohol use.

The potential value of such surveys is equaled by the danger of developing or using them inappropriately. Since it takes time to develop, edit, and distribute a valid survey and then tabulate the results, the alleged need for one can be used as a delaying tactic to block real action. *The task force should not acquiesce to a suggestion that further action on programs be postponed until the survey has been completed and the results have been thoroughly interpreted.* Academic quibbling over the validity of the survey and red-herring arguments about what the information means and how it should be applied may also arise. For example, if survey scores fall below the national average in regard to the number of drug users, someone may ask, "Does this mean that we don't have a drug problem or need drug programs?" If the scores are above average, someone else may ask, "How do we know that the test is valid?" Remember, the survey and the resultant data are tools; don't let them become political footballs!

Since almost all children attend schools, schools are a logical place to distribute a survey. However, the task force may need to obtain approval from—

- an internal review committee, including top administrators;
- a reading specialist who can judge whether the terms and syntax used are appropriate for specific grade levels;
- a parent review committee; and
- the parents of all students who will take the survey. (Parents should be told that the survey is optional and anonymous and that they can review the survey if they are willing to come to the school to look it over.)

There is no reason to hire a consultant to develop a new survey from scratch. The basic questions needed for a survey of drug use patterns in the community have already been developed and tested in a variety of contexts. State and federal agencies have forms available that should resolve most of the potential problems regarding the survey.

Interviewing key persons. Some of the most effective and persuasive information collected in any needs assessment comes from interviews with key persons in the system or community. There is a wide selection of prospective interviewees from which to choose: teachers, school counselors and administrators, judges, juvenile justice workers, mental health care counselors, child welfare workers, police officers, parents, clergy, physicians, nurses, psychologists, and recovering kids.

A sample interview form is provided in Appendix C. Task force members can use the questions as they appear on this form, adapt them to suit their purposes, or write new questions. Some questions may not be relevant for all

Beware of red-herring arguments and academic quibbling over the survey of drug use patterns.

interviewees, but if task force members intend to ask the same question of several people, they must be certain that it *is* the same question. For example, they should not ask one person how many young people he or she knows personally who are using chemicals and then ask another what percentage of young people in the community he or she thinks might be using. If task force members don't adhere to a specific interview format, the editing and interpretation of responses will be a nightmare.

Surveying social service providers. This phase of the needs assessment is crucial to program design. Regardless of the task force's focus of concern or specific program goals, its members should become thoroughly familiar with—

- assessment and referral services for chemical, family, and mental health problems;
- services directly related to adolescent and adult alcohol and drug use, including awareness and education resources, inpatient and outpatient treatment, aftercare programs, halfway houses, and long-term residential programs;
- family counseling services;
- psychological and psychiatric services; and
- other community services that may be helpful with such program development tasks as general planning and evaluation, design and production of educational materials, funding, and training.

The task force may not have to do all the digging on its own. Some agency or person in the community may already have compiled a comprehensive list of social services. Many school districts publish resource guides for area families. In communities and school districts where there are no such directories, task forces often make the compilation of a social services list one of their first projects.

Some communities are served by an information and referral (I&R) agency. I&R agencies act as clearinghouses for information about social services available in a specific area; they are not assessment and referral agencies, which do evaluations of individual clients. If such an agency is unavailable, county welfare departments, other social service agencies, and the United Way provide similar information.

In compiling a list of available resources, task force members should ask clergy, police officers, physicians, and social workers for recommendations. They should look in the Yellow Pages of local telephone directories under such headings as Alcoholics Anonymous, alcoholism information and treatment, clinics, drug abuse and addiction, marriage and family counselors, mental health centers, physicians and surgeons, psychiatrists and psychotherapists, psychologists, social service organizations, and social workers. Whenever they contact service providers, they should ask staff members to direct them to similar or related services.

After the task force has identified all potential service providers available, it must determine which of them can best meet the needs of the proposed program. This is usually done by visiting them and asking others in the community about the quality of services rendered. When a task force member contacts an agency, he or she must identify what services are offered under what conditions. He or she must also make note of who is and is not eligible, what fees are charged, and whether or not insurance policies cover the cost of services. The agency's source of funds must also be ascertained. Many agencies supported by tax revenues must meet certain conditions in order to receive their allocation. Such conditions might stipulate that an agency provide certain types of services or serve certain groups of people from specific geographical areas. Some communities have surveyed consumers to determine whether they were satisfied with the treatment they received. In summary, task force members should try, in any way they can, to determine the quality of services being offered by the agency. If the agency is not doing what it is funded to do, the task force may have the right to request changes.

A sample form for keeping track of basic information about service providers in a community is provided in Appendix D. In addition to using this form, task force members can make notes about their general impressions of each provider. What are its apparent strengths and weaknesses? If an agency is currently geared toward helping adults, how does its staff feel about working with adolescents? How does its staff feel about working closely with the system being approached by the task force? Does the agency adhere to a distinct model or philosophy of treatment? The answer to this last question, of course, has particular relevance. If the task force plans to set up a school-based program with the philosophical goal of changing adolescent norms to *no drug use*, its members probably would find it difficult to work with service providers that either allow "responsible" use by their clients or assume that all drug use is a sign of chemical dependency and calls for immediate inpatient treatment. The task force should know the score before it counts on working with any service provider.

Step eight: Write a program proposal

After the task force has completed the needs assessment, the next step on the agenda is to write a program proposal. Actually, these two agenda tasks are rarely done in chronological order. Most task forces that do a needs assessment before they approach the governing body simultaneously generate program ideas and develop means of implementing them.

Whatever the timing, eventually the task force must marshall its information and ideas and put them on paper. However, the task force need not use every fact, statute, statistic, and interview anecdote at its disposal unless it anticipates fierce resistance that might be swayed by massive documentation. It makes sense to save some persuasive material to be used in presenting the proposal to the governing body.

The program proposal should outline only the most salient and concise information: (1) background (how the idea for the program developed); (2) general definition of the problem of adolescent drug and alcohol use; (3) specific findings of the needs assessment; (4) general goals of the program; (5) organizational considerations; (6) sequence of program implementation; (7) staffing; (8) program costs and funding plans; and (9) criteria and projected date for program evaluation.

The task force may use the sample proposal outline presented in Appendix E, but first it should determine if the governing body favors a different format. If so, the task force should write its proposal in that format.

Step nine: Obtain financial support

Money is always a big issue. Initially, a program should be funded by several sources. Such fund raising requires much time, legwork, and politicking, but it yields more than money. By seeking even temporary financial support from private foundations, civic action groups, fraternal and sororal organizations, businesses and industry, churches, and individuals, the task force introduces these potential sponsors to a different, better way of looking at drug programming for the community.

Although a program can be started on the proverbial "wing and a prayer" with temporary support, it won't survive without a stable financial base. While private foundation and federal grants are of great help, we've all seen too many programs rise up, soar, wobble, and fail on the unpredictable currents of grant funds. When the grantor decides to support some new project, old programs fall apart.

The solution is to secure permanent backing from the governing body. Most programs, however, are caught between the infamous "rock and a hard place": A program won't last without the financial support of the governing body, which is more likely to make such a commitment if it doesn't have to pay the whole tab immediately. What does the task force ask for, then?

The first strategy is to convince the governing body to pay for *some* part of the program the first year. The amount of support is usually specified in the program proposal and, however small, brings the governing body closer to feeling invested in the total program. It pays to decide which facet of the program is most compatible with the present interests of these board or committee members. For example, a task force could ask a school board to send a key coach or counselor to a training workshop to learn about adolescent drug use, abuse, and dependency so that he or she could share this information with other school staff members. The board thus would be funding that part of the program that benefits its own interests, regardless of whether or not it is fully committed to the total program initially.

The second strategy is to persuade the governing body to

make funds for the program a line item in its system's overall budget. Once a program has been integrated into this budget, it has taken a giant step toward attaining long-term viability because the sponsoring system is now definitely invested in it.

The task of fund raising entails more than soliciting money, however. A common and legitimate complaint of sponsors is that after they've given their money away, they hear nothing from the grantees until more money is needed. Whether the task force receives an outright grant, matching funds, or support-in-kind aid, one of the members should take the time to tell the sponsor about the program's successes and failures. For example, if a business sponsors the training of local professionals or school staff members, the trainees should report back to the business about the impact that this experience had on them and the program.

At least in the beginning, drug programs should be funded by several sources.

Step ten: Present the program proposal

Presenting the program proposal to the governing body for approval involves politicking pure and simple. At this point, the task force's objectives are to follow due procedures, to communicate concerns and information, and to push for recognition and approval from those who can help implement solutions to the problem. Only task force members can answer these questions: How does the governing body process proposals and make decisions? How much resistance do we expect to encounter? Which board or committee members are most open to our ideas and concerns? Are any of them likely to staunchly support or vehemently oppose us?

Although I can offer no hard-and-fast formula for handling the politicking needed to win approval, I suggest that the task force be prepared to approach the governing body formally on at least three occasions and informally on many others.

Three formal meetings. As I've stated, the *first meeting* concerns the task force's request to be sanctioned as an ad hoc committee to investigate the problem and possible solutions.

In the *second meeting*, the task force formally asks the governing body to hold a special three-hour meeting so that it can present its research findings and proposal. This tactic keeps the task force's presentation from being scheduled into a regular board or committee meeting as just another item on an already crowded agenda. A special meeting ensures that the task force will command the governing body's full attention and increase its chances of achieving its goals.

Some lobbying may be necessary before the task force makes this formal request. Many task forces have found it advantageous to contact each member of the governing body individually, disclose to him or her the general findings of the needs assessment and the basic content of the proposal, and then ask him or her to support a request for a special meeting. In fact, many task forces have learned not to make a formal request for a special meeting until they know, from informal contact, that they have the necessary support.

Remember, the purpose of this second meeting is to convince the governing body not of the need for a program but of the need for a special three-hour meeting. This is a limited goal.

The content of and the time needed for the *third, special meeting* depend on the focus and scope of the proposal. The task force's general goals in this meeting are to—

- explain the concepts of chemical use, abuse, and dependency;
- describe the effects of drug use on children, adolescents, parents, and families; on the system directed by the governing body; and on the community;
- relate the specific impact of adolescent drug use on the community (based on survey responses and interviews); and
- present the program proposal.

The task force may also invite key persons from the community to relate their special insights into the problem of adolescent drug use. During needs assessment interviews, interviewees should be asked whether they would be willing, at a later date, to share their knowledge with the governing body. Such testimonies can be most effective.

Three hours is a ballpark figure, but it certainly is not too much time to request if the task force plans to cover all these points. A good moderator can set the pace at this third meeting.

Need for a two-year commitment. Included in the proposal presentation should be the request for, at the very least, a two-year commitment from the governing body. Such a request may not apply if the focus of concern is limited, for example, to a short-lived volunteer project. For a school-based early-intervention program, however, a two-year commitment is the minimum. A modest intervention and referral program can be set up in a few months, but it will take time before people start using program services to capacity. This is a marathon, not a 100-yard dash. The task force should not permit anyone to blow the whistle before the program can hit its stride. If someone says, "We'll give you one year to prove to us that this will work," back away. Don't compromise on this issue. Incorporate a two-year commitment into the proposal and be firm about it.

NEED FOR PATIENCE AND PERSEVERANCE

So what happens after the task force has dazzled the governing body with thorough research, undeniably valid testimonies, and an exemplary program proposal? It approves the proposal immediately, right? Wrong. Administrative bodies are often surprisingly quick to reject an idea, but they are slow to commit to drug programs. The task force should take this part of the game in stride—and be prepared with its own strategy.

You and the other task force members *will* gain the approval you need if you keep pressing for action. Be patient. It may take months or even a year or two to get a go-ahead. You may have to meet with the members of the governing body several times. You may have to call in a well-respected consultant to

Administrative bodies can be surprisingly quick to reject an idea but slow to commit to drug programs. Persevere!

back up the task force's recommendations. You may have to persuade some key members of the governing body to attend training. Without being angry, judgmental, or accusatory, you may have to penetrate a thick barrier of denial by firmly confronting the governing body with new facts as they emerge. And new facts *will* emerge, for without programs that intervene on and prevent drug use and abuse, kids and families will continue to live with pain, dysfunction, and even death.

Unfortunately, countless school boards have steadfastly refused to see or help solve the adolescent drug problem until faced with a crisis: kids dying in a drunken-driving accident, a drug-using student committing suicide, or the entire football team being busted at a beer-and-pot party. As callous as this may sound, a crisis can be useful. It can overcome the barrier of denial. If it takes a crisis to awaken the community, use it as an opportunity to press for programs. As any professional who works with alcoholics knows, a crisis is a legitimate and appropriate time to intervene.

A word to the wise here: Support sometimes comes easily after a crisis has shaken the community, but all too often it is short-lived. Once the shock wears off and the collective guilt has been assuaged by a new program or two, you and the other task force members may find yourselves talking to the walls again . . . unless you have proceeded with your plans as originally devised and presented.

Community mobilization against adolescent drug use consists of some basic steps that can lead to success—if all goes as planned. However, more variables than any one person or group can predict or control also come into play. Do not be discouraged, then, if things do not move in a straight line. Each person reached during the process of mobilizing the community in turn will reach out to others. Little by little the community will change.

Sweeping change occurs only partly by design. If you work on intervening in the key systems in the community, if you make connections with others on the basis of your shared concern for kids, and if you are wise and humble enough to know that neither you nor your programs can solve the whole problem, then your efforts may very well trigger an amazing chain reaction. You may well ask, "How in the world did all of

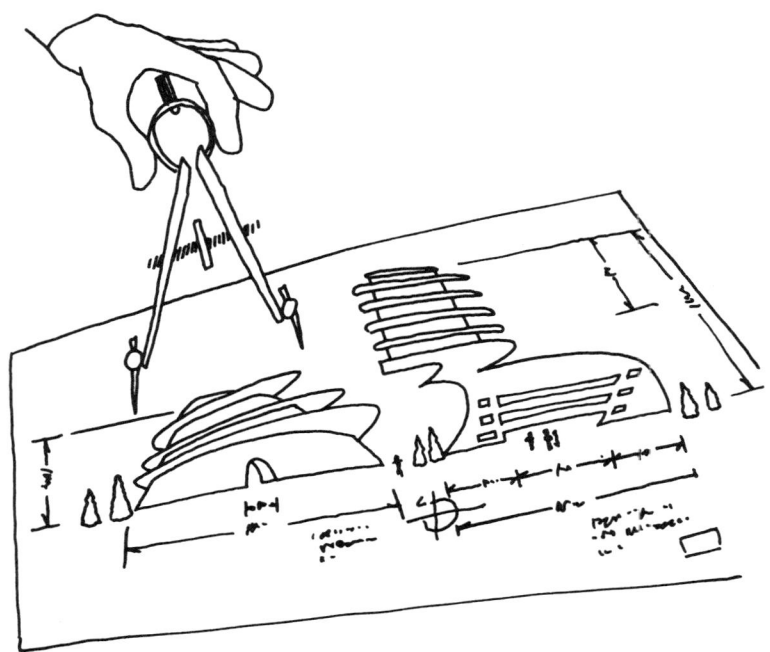

Sweeping change occurs only partly by design. Humble efforts can have amazing results.

this happen? How did we get here?" Well, one individual working alone is better than none, but ten individuals working together have more than ten times the impact. That's synergy: the whole being greater than the sum of its parts. It's an alliance for change.

* * * * * * * *

Once the program proposal has been granted approval, work on the nitty-gritty details of implementing an early-intervention program can begin. In the next chapter, I'll describe the rationale for and the internal organization of a school-based early-intervention program.

CHAPTER FIVE

Focus on School Drug Programs

The pain of the adolescent drug problem, with its attendant fear, loneliness, and frustration, bites deeply into the heart of every parent who has had to face the nightmare of family life without trust, without understanding. The pain and frustration are not confined to the family, however. They spread far beyond the family and touch many others in the community. The daily lives of school personnel in particular are strongly affected by the many drug problems with which they must deal, directly or indirectly, on a regular basis. The determination to change "the way things are" often begins when teachers, counselors, custodians, principals, and specialists decide that they have had enough of the eerie silence that shrouds the problem and are tired of feeling frustrated and helpless.

The following scenario is typical of many after-school meetings of school staff members concerned about the situation they all face every workday:

> "I came to this meeting," says the young chemistry teacher, "because I have so many kids this year who have something on their minds that keeps them from paying attention and doing their work. I can't reach them! Is it my fault? Some kids will always be bored, I know, but why so many this year? They *all* can't be doing drugs . . . can they?"
>
> "Let me tell you something," says the custodian, who has put in more years at the high school than anyone else in the room. "You teachers never set foot in the kids' johns anymore. You don't know what all goes on in there."

The determination to change "the way things are" often begins when school staff members meet to explore solutions to the problem.

The assistant principal interrupts: "I've told the school board for two years now that if something isn't done about the number of kids who come to school stoned and then get high again over lunch hour, we might as well give up trying to teach them anything. Babysitters, that's all we are for these kids." Looking around the room, he adds, "And we aren't very good babysitters at that. We all avoid that northside door and we all know why."

"So? What can we do about it?" asks a history teacher. "Principal Maloney has tied our hands and the superintendent has his in a knot. No one who could do something wants to do anything!"

"That's not quite true," the school counselor protests. "I've talked to Maloney about this myself because . . . well, I don't know if I should tell all of you this, but 14 seniors and 2 juniors have come to me already this year about drug problems of one kind or another."

"Fourteen! That's 5% of the senior class. Who are they?" asks the assistant principal.

"Some of them you already know about, I'm sure, but I promised I wouldn't identify them. Besides, some are just worried about their friends and won't even tell me their names. I didn't know what to do, so I went to Maloney. I think he'd like to do something—*if* he had the money," replies the school counselor.

"I wonder if money is really the issue," comments the social studies teacher who called the meeting. "My sister-in-law teaches at a school where the staff runs a drug program during school hours."

"How could we do that? We aren't drug counselors!" insists a math teacher. "Besides, we're overscheduled as it is."

"Well, her whole community is behind it, I guess. Teachers don't treat the kids; they just identify the ones who need help. Volunteers and parents help the school staff, and they've got a network set up with a lot of social service agencies," says the social studies teacher.

"I think you should find out more about that," the assistant principal suggests. "And let's meet again in two weeks—*with* Maloney this time. We've got all the concern and talent we need right here in this room. Maybe we could get something going here if we had some community support."

"Well, I know a couple of drug counselors from the county," says the school counselor. "They've wanted to get the schools involved for a long time."

"And you know," says the basketball coach, "just the other day I heard about this parents group . . . ."

This meeting is typical in that frustration and, at first, a sense of hopelessness are so apparent. What is atypical, perhaps, is that someone at the meeting knows a teacher elsewhere who is already working in a successful school-based drug program that has community support. Without the injection of hope provided by the example of another school district that has chosen not to run away from its problems, the meeting just described could well have degenerated into a blaming game ending with the loud chorus, "Ain't it a shame?"

Chapters Five and Six offer hope and direction to those of you who are looking for a way to deal with the drug problems in your schools. These two chapters are a culmination of all the information that you've read in the preceding chapters, just as the specific program ideas presented here are the result of many years of working with communities to find positive ways to help young people. Different people in different communities ask the same questions: "How can we accomplish the most for the least time, money, and human energy? What kind of programming creates the most leverage in working for change? Where should these programs be based? Who should run them? What does it take to be effective for once?"

In my experience, the most effective plan of action in many, many communities has been the *school-based early-intervention program*, which is designed to identify students with drug-related problems and refer them for help to counseling and treatment services. In this chapter, we'll look at the rationale for basing early-intervention programs in the schools and the usual way in which these programs are organized internally. This material is not meant exclusively for educators. Most of the concepts and techniques of school-based early-intervention programs also apply to those programs based in courts, mental health centers, or other systems.

RATIONALE FOR SCHOOLS' INVOLVEMENT

Drug problems *do* affect schools directly. School staff members—from the administrators to the teachers to the nurses to the part-time office workers—are all on the front line; they see what is happening to students, to their own attitudes, and to education in general. Although effective early-intervention programs can be set up in or with the help of many systems—and many different systems *should* be involved in drug education and prevention programs—I firmly believe that a school-based early-intervention program provides the greatest leverage in working for change in the community.

Like most institutions having a long tradition of great social responsibility, schools usually aren't quick to change, and most of them aren't inventive. However, they are adept at adapting ideas that have proved successful elsewhere. Furthermore, many educators will take action once they see a reasonable, clearly defined role for schools in the intervention process.

Schools' role in early intervention

The primary advantage of basing early-intervention and prevention programs in the schools can be summarized in six words: *School is where the kids are!* What other system has contact with almost every young person in the community? Certainly not the juvenile justice system or the churches or the family social service agencies. Where do kids buy, sell, and learn to use alcohol and other drugs? They certainly don't hang out at church getting high and trading drugs. School is the place where they share ideas, experiences, and plans; where they teach one another that drug use is OK and "cool."

School is also the place where a trained staff educates and nurtures young people and monitors their growth until age 18. After age 18, of course, these young adults go their separate ways—some go to college, some work, some enlist in the armed services, and some marry and start a family. Clearly, if we want to reach as many kids as we can, school is *the* place to do it most efficiently and effectively.

The aforementioned pragmatic advantages of school-based programs are probably obvious to those of us who think comprehensively about adolescent alcohol and drug programming. There are, however, many teachers and administrators who continue to argue against schools' involvement in drug issues and programs. For some, the argument is a matter of who is at fault: "Schools didn't cause

School staff members are all on the front line; they see the effects of student drug use in their classrooms and on their own attitudes.

the drug problem; why should schools be held responsible for solving it?" For others, it is philosophical: "The purpose of schools is to teach, not provide therapy!" The latter argument has been heard with increasing frequency in the past few years in the wake of budget cutbacks and the clarion call for schools to return to teaching the basics.

If you encounter such resistance as you push for school-based programs, it's important to get a sense of its origin. It could stem from a fear of being blamed for the problem just for showing an interest in working on it. If so, make it clear not only that schools are *not* held solely responsible for solving a problem that they indeed did not cause but also that other systems and agencies in the community network will support their efforts. If resistance on the part of teachers stems from a sincere desire to focus their talents and efforts on only those jobs for which they were trained, then read on, because the educational roles in early-intervention and prevention programs dovetail with educators' traditional roles and make appropriate use of their skills.

To those who insist that the activities involved in implementing a school-based early-intervention program go far beyond the schools' role, I would like to point out that teachers and other school staff members have always encouraged students to grow physically, intellectually, and emotionally. In school, students are praised for improvements in academic work and are urged to participate in clubs, sports, and a myriad of other activities. In short, educators try to create a supportive environment in which young people can take risks and grow. By developing awareness programs and clear-cut policies and procedures on drugs, by using services in the community appropriately, and by providing support for students who are trying to make changes, schools are simply doing what needs to be done to create an environment conducive to academic and personal growth.

Again, don't waste time arguing. If you've presented research findings and the program proposal to the school board, if you've been patient and perseverant, if you've lobbied and politicked and the school board still won't approve the program, save your strength. Don't become ensnared in a philosophical debate that you can't win—let the historians of the philosophy of education work it out. Help to initiate strong early-intervention and prevention programs in another system—for example, a local youth agency, a church group, or the juvenile justice department. Success there will supply the leverage needed to intervene in the schools. Remember, most elements of the early-intervention program to be described in this chapter are applicable to many systems, not just schools.

EARLY-INTERVENTION PROGRAMMING

Early-intervention programming is a strategy that allows schools to first help the young people (and their families) who need it most and then work to prevent other students from starting to use drugs. Drug-related problems come in many different packages. By means of school-based programs, staff members should eventually be able to identify and refer for help—

- the senior whose chemical abuse is destroying his chances for physical, psychological, emotional, and spiritual growth and possibly endangering his life;
- the fifth grader who is learning self-destructive behavioral patterns from her alcoholic parents; and
- the student of any age who, in bowing to peer pressure, is making unwise and possibly dangerous decisions about drugs because of misinformation and the need to be accepted.

Early-intervention programs are designed so that *all* young people affected by drug or alcohol use can be identified and referred to services that can help them *before* their problems become serious. This is part of the intervention-to-prevention approach: Concentrate on intervening on junior and senior high students, many of whom will already have started using drugs regularly, and then extend the program downward to students in the elementary grades. As soon as possible, initiate a strong prevention program in the lower grades and extend it upward. Eventually, each program will encompass students at all grade levels throughout the school district. Remember to start small and make good on limited goals. Then, even the most reluctant, cynical, or unconvinced of the school staff members will see that it is possible to help students with drug problems. If you start small, you have a better chance of succeeding than if you start too big and unexpected obstacles force you to retrench. Limited funds and staff time also prove to be less of a problem when goals are manageable.

A small-but-growing program can also become a powerful catalyst for involving other schools and other school districts. Understandably, people may not want to risk acknowledging and confronting a drug problem in the schools if they fear that a program might cost a million dollars and prove worthless and embarrassing in the end. However, if they witness an efficient early-intervention program having a positive impact in another community, they are more likely to decide to set up one of their own.

INTERNAL ORGANIZATION

The internal organization of a school-based early-intervention program consists of (1) the core team, (2) the program coordinator, and (3) the advisory board. Very small school districts find one core team and one program coordinator sufficient for the entire district; larger districts need a core team in each building.

Much like participation in interest groups and task forces, involvement with a core team must be voluntary. A firm commitment from school administrators and the cooperation and commitment of school staff members are crucial to the longevity and effectiveness of school-based programs. Don't accept school staff members appointed or commanded by the administration to take part. Again, start small, with whatever concern exists and build from there; don't try to legislate cooperation.

Remember, the schools take primary responsibility not for solving the community's drug problem but for implementing their own early-intervention programs. Although school staff members definitely need the assistance of parents, community volunteers, and social service professionals, this program must become an integral part of the school system's educational package. While parents *could* handle the awareness and education presentations, it would be difficult to mesh their efforts with school curriculum and other school activities. While community volunteers *could* organize and maintain the preliminary assessment and referral services, they would have a hard time identifying the students who need help because they lack daily contact with them. While social service professionals *could* facilitate the in-school support groups, most school administrators would be very reluctant to have personnel without teaching certificates running programs in their schools. Thus, the core team members and the program coordinator should be people who work within the school system.

The core team

Once an early-intervention effort has been initiated in a school district, a number of staff members usually voice an interest in working in the program. Some or all of those who are interested enough to become regular members of a core team may constitute an ideal team. If not, you can actively recruit certain staff members to achieve a more effective balance of talents. While you shouldn't force people to serve on the core team, you can entice or cajole them into joining your ranks.

Here are some guidelines for the recruitment and selection of core team members:

- *Assemble an interdisciplinary team.* Do all you can to ensure that the team includes teachers from several disciplines, a counselor, an administrator, a coach, a nurse, and a noncertificated staff member. This mix provides a balanced approach to program planning and helps to defuse fear and resentment of the program.
- *Select individuals who are respected and trusted by students and other staff members.* Generally, no one person will command the respect and trust of every student or every staff member, but every student and every staff member should respect and trust at least one of the core team members. Select the core team carefully so that you can reach the entire student body and, perhaps more important, the entire school staff.
- *Encompass a range of talents.* Make certain that the team possesses a broad range of talents. Obviously, you'll need team members who like intense, direct contact with students

The internal organization of a school-based program consists of the core team, the program coordinator, and the advisory board.

to facilitate student support groups. In addition, you'll need detail-oriented members to keep records, members who have good rapport with the rest of the school staff and can explain the program and the procedures to follow in specific cases, and members who are effective public speakers.

- *Include school staff members only.* Don't select anyone from outside the school system for the core team, unless helping professionals are an intrinsic part of the district's daily operations. This guideline is of special importance because core team members often must deal with confidential information, which can be shared with other school staff members on a need-to-know basis but cannot be shared with persons outside the school system unless they first go through the proper channels. Although students can't participate in core team activities that involve confidential

information about the problems of other students, they can do some projects for or with the core team. (Because confidentiality is a matter of great concern, an in-depth discussion of it concludes this chapter.)
- *Keep people with drug problems off the core team.* Don't try to intervene on a staff member's chemical abuse by pressing him or her to attend a training workshop or to serve on the core team.
- *Ask for a two-year commitment.* Avoid selecting school staff members who refuse to commit themselves to a two-year tenure on the team. You probably will lose some members who will make the commitment in good faith but burn out after several months and beg off. Nevertheless, you can count on the majority of committed staff members to serve for two years.
- *Avoid the all-purpose zealot.* Don't load the team with staff members noted for their vehement support of every cause that comes down the pike—from saving the whales to halting the use of nuclear energy to promoting the latest educational fad—especially if their habitual zealotry leaves others cold.
- *Recruit far in advance of the new school year.* Instead of waiting for the opening of school to convince certain staff members that they would find various program activities worthwhile and fulfilling if they joined the core team, begin recruiting them during the winter or early spring of the preceding year. It stands to reason that no matter how interested a teacher may be, if she already supervises the school newspaper and is involved in a tutorial project for a community development agency, she is just too busy to join the core team at a moment's notice. However, if you approach her this year about being on the team next year, you stand a much better chance of recruiting her.

Core team tasks. The core team is primarily responsible for seeing that program activities are carried out. Its tasks are as follows:

- *Liaison.* Core team members act as contacts for other school staff members, students, parents, and social service professionals in the community when they need help with

personal problems, advice about dealing with someone who may have a drug problem, or simple clarification of program policies and procedures.
- *Preliminary assessment.* The core team gathers data to determine whether a student referred to it because of an academic or behavioral problem, drug-related or not, would benefit from in-school services such as a student support group or whether he or she should undergo an in-depth assessment conducted by a social service professional in the community. The core team also establishes formal and informal procedures for accepting referrals; for checking one staff member's observations against those of other teachers, coaches, and administrators; and for deciding what action is most appropriate at the time. Not every person on a core team has to be directly involved in this preliminary assessment process. However, each core team member is

Seek core team members who are respected and trusted. Avoid the all-purpose zealot, especially if his or her vehemence leaves others cold.

responsible for ensuring that adequate preliminary assessment services are being offered.

- *Administrative record keeping.* A core team member must keep records on individual students, the number and type of referrals made to the program, the disposition of referrals, and the general scope and types of program activities in operation. These records include confidential case material needed for working with individual students and aggregate data needed for program evaluation.
- *Development of policies and procedures.* The core team reviews and revises the school's policies and procedures regarding students who are in trouble because of drug use or some other problem. Such policies and procedures should address not only students' behaviors (for example, what to do when intoxication is suspected) but also such issues as how to release students from class to attend a support group and how to give a student credit for class assignments completed while he or she is in a treatment center.
- *Planning of awareness and education presentations.* Core team members help design awareness and education presentations for staff, parents, and students.
- *Curriculum consultation.* A representative from the core team should advise the district curriculum committee on matters and materials relevant to student drug and alcohol use and early-intervention programming.

Core team meetings and training. Core team members should meet at least once a week. In addition, a half-day meeting should be scheduled at least once each quarter so that the team can handle all the issues that have not been attended to during the hustle and bustle of weekly problem solving.

It is essential that core team members be trained, preferably in the manner recommended in Chapter Four. Community Intervention, Inc., and other private and public organizations offer seminars, workshops, and summer courses. Interested but inexperienced core team members can learn about drug and alcohol use and abuse, the role of the schools in intervention and prevention, effective methods of working with parents and people from other systems, preliminary assessment of drug problems, and facilitation of student support groups. Such training also provides participants with a shared vision about the purpose of their program and a common set of concepts and techniques with which to realize that vision.

In an ongoing early-intervention program, the need for training recurs periodically. Program growth demands more service, and more service means more staff members must become actively involved in the program. The training given to additional staff must be congruent with past training efforts. The commonality of the training experience among staff members is essential to the continuity of the program, its goals, procedures, and practices. The spirit infused during training will be reinforced for each core team member as new members are added to the team. The more unified team members are in terms of personal rapport and professional methods, the better able they are to deal with the delusion, denial, fear, and other forms of resistance that are commonplace among school staff members.

Core teams must be prepared to work with less than 100% support at first. Sometimes this means carrying on in a highly politicized atmosphere and being on guard against maneuvers meant to undermine the program. Sometimes it means countering more diffuse resistance. To be patient and sympathetic yet persevere in the face of such obstacles is the challenge confronting every core team member. Satisfaction comes in winning support by proving able to help students whom others have not been able to reach.

The program coordinator

The program coordinator oversees all core team tasks. He or she may be a member of a single core team in a small school district or a free-floating member of several core teams in a large district. In the very early stages of a program, the coordinator can often combine coordination duties with his or her regular job. As a program grows, however, the coordination duties become increasingly more demanding, political, and sophisticated. At a certain point, they require the attention of a full-time coordinator.

In most cases, the person chosen to be the coordinator will have been directly involved with students as a counselor or a

At a certain point in a program's development, the position of coordinator becomes a full-time job.

member of the core team. As program coordinator, he or she is expected to consult with core team members who need advice concerning particular students and to review all outside referrals to ensure that each student has received the appropriate service. In addition, the coordinator may take on any number of other duties, depending on the structure of the program and the district in which the program functions.

To a large extent, the position of a program coordinator mirrors the position of an athletic director. In a small school district, the athletic director usually teaches, coaches, schedules conference games, reviews the athletic budget, and performs other administrative duties. In a large district, administrative duties demand the athletic director's full-time attention. Similarly, the program coordinator of a small early-intervention program works primarily as a teacher or counselor and administers the program as well. For a larger program, the job of the coordinator is more complex and thus demands full-time attention.

The following job description details the duties of an early-intervention program coordinator in a Minnesota school district with 13,000 students:

1. The Coordinator of the Student Assistance Program will work directly with the Director of Secondary Education.
2. The Coordinator will perform the responsibilities as listed:

- Disseminate information about the program to school staff.
- Arrange for the training of school staff and core team members.
- Work with the core team in each building and coordinate the activities of all the core teams.
- Serve as a resource person to building staffs to assist in developing procedures for working with students who have drug-related and other personal problems.
- Serve as a resource person to building staffs in establishing support groups and Alateen groups.
- Plan and coordinate in-service education for staff members and educational sessions for spouses, families, students, and the community.
- Establish and coordinate procedures for communicating with parents, law enforcement agencies, and human service organizations.
- Advise the administration of policies and procedures regarding chemical use.
- Work with the adult education coordinator in establishing classes on parenting and identification of chemical use and related problems.
- Update school personnel on available social services in the community.
- Monitor the continuum of intervention, treatment, and aftercare services available to students.
- Serve as a consultant to the curriculum planning committee.
- Serve as a consultant to school nurses, counselors, and other personnel and to parents.
- Perform other tasks and responsibilities as assigned by the Director of Secondary Education.

Again, not all program coordinators will need to shoulder such extensive responsibilities. I just wanted to illustrate the degree of hard work and dedication that this position can entail.

The advisory board

Some advisory boards take a very political stance, while others focus primarily on the quality of service given to students. The makeup and functions of the advisory board depend on the profile of the community and the way in which the program evolves.

To be most effective, the advisory board should consist of a wide range of concerned persons from the school district and the community—parents, school board members, businesspersons, clergy, police officers, juvenile justice workers, helping professionals, students, and others.

The board's functions include acting as a liaison between the school program and the social service agencies that are or could be assisting the program and the community as a whole. The board may also help to coordinate the activities of the school-based program with those of other programs and spearhead additional mobilization efforts in the community. By its very existence as a board made up of community members, it also conveys the message that while the school is doing something about the problem of drug use among students, the school itself should not and cannot be held solely responsibile for solving it.

Fund raising is another important function of the advisory board. As discussed later, it is essential that the school district make certain program expenses regular line items in the district's budget. However, certain expenses, such as those incurred in publishing a pamphlet, sending a coach to a training workshop, or cosponsoring a local workshop with neighboring communities, can be paid for with donations from individuals, civic action groups, and businesses in the community. Advisory board members can be extremely helpful in appealing to potential donors.

CONFIDENTIALITY

Confidentiality is an ethical, professional, and legal issue. Focusing exclusively on legal matters can be both misleading and counterproductive. Many schools begin a consideration of the confidentiality issue by bringing in a lawyer to explain the various laws applicable to confidentiality and to summarize past interpretations and future implications of those laws. It doesn't take much of a legal mind, however, to inform teachers that they could be sued *for* revealing information that students tell them about their drug use and *for not* revealing the same information when a student's life is in danger. Raising the possibility, however unlikely, of legalistic double binds only stimulates anxiety and does nothing to show staff members how to approach the issue of confidentiality in an ethical, professionally competent manner that is congruent with existing laws.

I do not mean to imply or promote a cavalier attitude concerning confidentiality. Sessions on confidentiality should be a regular part of any training program for all teachers, especially those working in early-intervention programs. School policies on confidentiality should be compatible in every respect with existing laws and binding regulations. For instance, staff members should never talk publicly about confidential information or allude openly to a student's participation in an early-intervention program. And, of course, a counselor's written remarks about a student's behavior in a support group should never appear in that student's permanent record file.

I do want to stress, however, that the great anxiety generated by the merest possibility of a lawsuit is unwarranted. Literally millions of students attend or have attended schools that sponsor early-intervention programs without hostile legal action being taken by parents.

Confidentiality versus discretion

Some parents groups are demanding that school staff members who discover that a student is using drugs must immediately report this fact to the student's parents. However, if schools were forced to accede to this demand for immediate, automatic reporting (which is very unlikely, since such a demand is probably incompatible with state and federal laws), the only option left to students would be to clam up with all school staff members. Thus, while proving their point about parental prerogatives, these parents could severely limit an early-intervention program's ability to identify and help young people with drug problems.

Allowing program staff members some discretion as to when they report a student's use of chemicals is advantageous for all involved. For instance, a student in a support group reveals that he is using alcohol again; however, he is not totally out of control and does not appear to be in a life-threatening situation. Given time, the facilitator and the other students in the group could get him to see the consequences of his actions and persuade him to tell his parents himself that he is drinking again. Trust in the program would be maintained, and the student would have a chance to act responsibly on his own behalf.

Discretion versus advocacy of "responsible" use

Some very effective counselors do not demand that a student who is just beginning individual counseling or has just joined an early-intervention group immediately agree to a written or oral contract stating that he or she will refrain from drug use. Does this stance constitute encouragement of "responsible" use of drugs? Hardly. There is a big difference between exercising some discretion in this matter and advocating responsible drug use.

Many staff members prefer to form an alliance with a young drug user before they demand an abstinence contract because they believe that without such rapport, the contract is meaningless. Their reasoning is simple: If the drug user has ignored school regulations, community norms, and state and federal laws, he or she can hardly be expected to take seriously another adult-imposed decree. If, however, a counselor and a drug user have formed a healthy alliance, an abstinence contract can prove very meaningful, for then it is based on—

- a shared perception that the young drug user is a person worthy of concern;
- an agreement that drugs have harmed him or her in specific ways; and
- an understanding that the purpose of counseling is to help, not to hurt or to discipline.

Important but nonconfidential information

In some school districts, student confidentiality is so closely protected that information revealed to a staff member can be relayed to parents only when the staff member deems the situation to be life-threatening. If this is the situation in your district, it may not be as much of an impediment as you may at first think. Much of the information needed to initiate an intervention is readily available to school staff and parents and does not come from self-disclosure by the student. For example, a drop in grades, regular absenteeism, and other observable behavioral cues do not fall under the jurisdiction of the laws on confidentiality. Often, such information is sufficient grounds for a school staff member to request an investigation of the problem. Furthermore, a counselor who has gained a student's trust can often persuade the student to tell his or her parents about his or her drug use.

Effects of being too confidential

In some schools, the rules on confidentiality are so strict that even teachers can't be told that a student is being treated for chemical dependency. Yes, of course, all his or her friends know. Yes, all the teachers will probably hear about it through the grapevine. Yes, the information will be distorted and in no way helpful in planning for his or her return to school after treatment. Such "confidentiality" fosters gossip and rumor, which perpetuates the stigma surrounding treatment and does nothing to help a young person in recovery.

Information sharing on need-to-know basis only

To preserve a student's privacy, only those school staff members who *need* to know about his or her drug problems or other personal problems should have access to such information. When a student returns to school following treatment for a drug problem, for instance, all the details do not have to be made known to all staff members. However, some teachers must be told about the classwork that the student completed while in treatment. Also, the general

When confidentiality rules are too strict, the grapevine takes over.

processes of a treatment program must be described to certain teachers if the student is to receive academic credit for having participated in various treatment groups. In many other instances, it is to the student's benefit to share information and to the student's detriment if information can't be shared. Most often, students themselves come to realize this and, with the support of a concerned adult, willingly share appropriate information with school staff members, parents, and friends.

Let me reiterate. It serves no good purpose to "clarify" the issue of confidentiality by means of a legalistic, technicality-ladened debate. Staff members should be rigorously trained to protect students' rights in an appropriate fashion and to know when and how to share information. Those regulations or interpretations of regulations that appear to block early-intervention strategy should be changed, at the state level if necessary, to ensure that students are not shortchanged by bureaucratic caprice.

* * * * * * * *

Together the core team, program coordinator, and advisory board of an early-intervention program provide a solid structure for program development and a broad base of support for the initiation and continuation of program activities. In the next chapter, we'll look at the dynamics of a school-based early-intervention program.

CHAPTER SIX

School Program Dynamics

The focus of school-based programs should be the implementation of the four key components of early-intervention programming described in Chapter Two: (1) awareness and education presentations, (2) identification and referral services, (3) continuum of counseling and treatment services, and (4) support groups and activities to help young people refrain from using alcohol and other drugs. In the following sections, I'll describe how these components are realized in a school-based early-intervention program.

AWARENESS AND EDUCATION

The sponsoring of awareness and education activities is a primary role of the schools in drug programming. Today, most school districts have some kind of drug and alcohol curriculum; even if they refuse to do more, they usually recognize that students must be taught about alcohol and other drugs as part of their preparation for adulthood. Education *is* the role of the schools: They have the mandate; they have the professional staff; they have the space. No other system in the community can do it better.

The ultimate goal of awareness and education presentations is simply to *help adults help kids make changes* in the way they view the use of alcohol and other drugs, in their own use habits, and in their reactions to drug use by those around them. Early-intervention educational efforts are more action-oriented and focused than most prevention curricula. Early-intervention programs emphasize drug problems to make people aware of those problems, to give people information about what they can do about them, and to motivate people to take action.

Target groups

When asked to name the primary target of early-intervention awareness and education efforts, most people would answer without hesitation, "Students, of course!" However, students are *not* the first target group. Past efforts have shown all too clearly that if we really want to help young people make changes, we must first reach adults—school staff members, parents, helping professionals, and volunteers.

If we start prematurely with students, two reactions are likely. First, some kids will blow us out of the water with ridicule and denial: "Who are these bozos, anyway? Drugs aren't that big a deal around here!" What's more, if at least some of the school staff members haven't been sensitized to the issue, the entire staff will be convinced that the kids are right. The staff won't understand the program, won't want to cooperate, and will pray fervently that the whole issue sinks 50 fathoms out of sight. Second, some kids will open up about their experiences, feelings, and concerns only to meet with denial and other defensive responses from adults. Students who are experimenting or are harmfully involved with drugs often do want to talk to someone. Contrary to popular opinion, the adults they approach often block communication by refusing to recognize the problem, by minimizing it, or by responding with phony and hysterical scare tactics. For a variety of reasons, then, the support and understanding of the school staff serve as the solid foundation on which to build the rest of the program's awareness and education activities. Thus, *school staff members* are the first target group.

The second target group is *parents*. Since they have primary responsibility for the welfare of their children, their understanding of early-intervention efforts is essential and their active participation in the program is invaluable. For without parental awareness, we may find ourselves in the difficult

To help kids make changes, we must first reach adults—school staff members, parents, professionals, and volunteers.

situation of trying to help children whose parents don't want our help.

The third target group is the *professional and volunteer community* upon which the school depends for services. Individuals from churches, businesses, civic action groups, law enforcement agencies, hospitals, and youth organizations as well as alcohol/drug abuse professionals should be made aware of the student drug problem and of the school's efforts to offer early-intervention services. School personnel tend to presume that social service professionals are already attuned to the basic concepts of intervention, but such is seldom the case. Some professionals do not consider drug use to be a serious problem; others see an alcoholic or addict in every student who so much as touches a chemical. Professionals and volunteers, then, must be exposed to some basic information about alcohol and drug problems and made aware of how their skills and services complement those of the early-intervention program staff.

Finally, the fourth target group is *students*. In addition to being taught about various topics directly related to drug use, students should be given the clear, honest impression that the adults in the school and community really believe in and support the school's policies on drug use and are ready, willing, and able to refer students to the program when necessary.

Basic content of presentations

The basic content of awareness and education presentations should address (1) the range and progression of drug use problems, (2) the "no-talk rule," (3) the difficulty posed by those adults and young people who enable drug users to continue using, and (4) the initial action steps that people can take when they encounter a drug problem.

These four categories serve as very broad guidelines for the basic content of awareness and education presentations. Undoubtedly, you may want to address other important educational issues during the year, but use these four categories as a general checklist. The question to ask is, Do these people really understand the problem of drug use, how it affects them, how they tend to prolong it, and how they can change things?

Range and progression of drug use problems. Most people do not know that there is a range of drug use problems and that behavior changes in broadly predictable ways as involvement with chemicals deepens. Many recognize only extreme cases of drug addiction or alcoholism, such as the skid-row bum whose life has been ruined by alcohol. They cannot see other, more subtle manifestations of drug abuse.

To be effective, awareness and education presentations must contain content that addresses this lack of knowledge. People must be taught how to identify and intervene on a wide variety of drug users, how to participate in program activities, and how to deal directly with students who are using drugs. For instance, we want people to know that we do not advocate incarcerating or referring for treatment every junior high school student who has had a beer. We also want people to know that we do not intend to ignore kids with apparently "minor" drug problems, since they may well be at high risk for becoming more enmeshed in drug use.

Through awareness and education presentations, people can also be taught to recognize signs and symptoms associated with chemical use and dependency. Some behaviors are directly related to chemical use. They include impaired coordination and speech, the smell of alcohol on the breath, red eyes, disheveled appearance, and erratic behavior—all of which point to recent intoxication—and exclusive association with a group of known heavy drug users. Other signs can be associated with a number of problems, not just the use of alcohol or other drugs. They include increased absenteeism, tardiness, and behavioral problems and poor academic performance. Any of these signs serves as an appropriate reason for referring a student to the school-based early-intervention program for preliminary assessment.

Bear in mind that in some schools the major barrier to referral is not that staff members and parents can't identify students who may have a drug problem but rather that they don't know they're expected to take action, don't know what action to take, and greatly fear what will happen if they do take action. Awareness and education efforts aimed at increasing the number of referrals to the early-intervention program should not be restricted to issues of identification alone. Just as important as the identification of possible drug problems are a clear explanation of the policies and procedures related to referral and assurances that staff members will be supported if they make a referral and that students referred for assistance will be handled in a beneficial manner.

"No-talk rule." In a well-planned drug awareness program, the effects of chemical use, abuse, and dependency on the families and friends of users are clearly described. This description should cover not only how a young drug user affects his or her siblings and parents but also how the children of drug users, especially alcoholics, are affected by their parents' problems. As Claudia Black states in her book *It Will Never Happen To Me!*, children of alcoholic parents learn three rules: Don't talk. Don't trust. Don't feel. The "no-talk rule" alone is a powerful impediment to change. It prevents people from sharing their perceptions and from developing any confidence in the accuracy of their perceptions. It further prevents people from developing mutual trust and understanding and blocks any chance of their joining together to consider positive action.

The no-talk rule extends beyond the immediate family. It affects friends, associates, teachers, school principals, and others, all of whom are genuinely unaware of how much they hurt themselves and the drug user by maintaining this conspiracy of silence. They are aware of the pain, frustration, fear, and helplessness they feel, but without some understanding of chemical abuse, they can never bring the source of these feelings into clear focus. By participating in awareness and education activities, they can learn to recognize and then break this rule and bring the barrier of denial tumbling down.

Enabling. The content of awareness and education presentations must also address the issue of enabling, that is, the well-meaning but misguided protection of users of alcohol or other drugs from the consequences of their destructive involvement with chemicals. Enabling allows drug users to avoid reality and thus to continue their self-destructive behavior.

Children of alcoholics grow up in families where three rules are primary: Don't talk. Don't trust. Don't feel.

Although the specific manifestations differ, the basic dynamics of and motivation for enabling are similar for many individuals. Most enablers think that if they don't "help" a spouse, a child, or a friend who gets into trouble because of his or her drug use—not getting to school on time, not reporting to work, being arrested for drunken driving or vandalism—matters can only get worse. In truth, matters will get worse *because* the enabler shields the drug user from the consequences of his or her behavior.

The barriers to recognizing enabling in ourselves are so strong that general discussions of the process do not suffice. All of us must learn to see the specific ways in which we, as parents, professionals, friends, and peers, minimize or deny the drug use we see around us. With the help of awareness and education presentations, we can remove the blinders.

Initial action steps. The fourth category of content essential to effective awareness and education presentations is a culmination of the first three: the initial action steps to take when a friend, a child, a parent, a client, or a student may be harmfully involved with alcohol or other drugs. Here again the information presented must be specific to be useful. For example, teachers should know the name of the staff member(s) they can contact when they have concerns. Students should know when, where, and how to meet with a counselor if they are worried about their own or someone else's drug use. Parents must know when and whom they can call and what phone number to call if they have a child in trouble.

All community members, especially school staff members, need to know what their alternatives are when they are concerned about someone. Although a school-based resource person may be available to provide this information, a number of individuals simply may not be comfortable contacting him or her. They should be given the names of social workers, counselors, and clergy who are competent in early-intervention techniques and other aspects of social service.

Content development and delivery

Teachers should take primary responsibility for the awareness

Teachers are well equipped to present information effectively and creatively.

and education presentations in an early-intervention program. There are two basic reasons for this. First, a school-based drug program must be incorporated into the school's staff-and-materials budget in as many ways as possible to ensure its longevity. Second, teachers have expertise in developing and presenting all types of course material. After receiving some specialized training, teachers are better equipped than most direct-service professionals to present information on drug use and abuse effectively and creatively to students and adults alike. As I've stated, however, primary responsibility is not sole responsibility. Assistance from parents, alcohol/drug abuse professionals, members of Alcoholics Anonymous and Al-Anon, volunteers from civic action groups, and others is crucial.

Typical awareness and education presentations include:

- mandatory in-service sessions for faculty and voluntary for-credit training sessions for all school staff members;
- chemical awareness days, parenting courses, evening training sessions, and intensive one-week workshops for parents, volunteers, and professionals; and
- regular classes, special prevention classes, chemical awareness fairs, and assemblies for students.

As the early-intervention program develops, situations that call for a change in content will no doubt arise. For example, core team members may notice that the staff neglects to refer minority students to the program. To counteract this situation, they could prepare and present material on the special problems of minority students to the entire staff. In this and hundreds of other ways, the nature of the early-intervention program and its progress in offering effective services will determine how to modify and improve the content of awareness and education presentations.

IDENTIFICATION AND REFERRAL

Identification and referral involves recognizing students who may need help and then making sure that they receive it. This component of early-intervention programming is well within the schools' traditional responsibilities and capabilities. Needed are:

- school staff members who are alert to possible problems, have some understanding of them, and can act in accordance with program policies and procedures; and
- some trained staff members on the core team who can screen students who have problems to determine whether they can be helped within the school system or should be referred to outside services.

Of all the components of school-based early-intervention programs, identification and referral is the component that usually elicits the most vociferous and adamant protests from staff members. "This isn't our job!" teachers exclaim. "Education programs, OK, but this is social work! We aren't the police. We aren't alcohol/drug abuse experts!" They often fear either that they'll be asked to catch students in the act of selling drugs or forced to add alcohol and drug counseling to their already heavy work loads. Neither fear is warranted.

Schools' role in identifying drug problems

Identification, by teachers, of possible drug-related problems requires no more of a rationale than does identification of possible vision and hearing disabilities. Obviously, teachers are not medical specialists, yet they have long accepted some responsibility for identifying these problems. The reason for this is pragmatic: A student with either of these problems simply can't learn as well as he or she could otherwise.

So what does a teacher do when he or she suspects that a student may have trouble seeing or hearing? Although procedures vary, the teacher usually refers the student and all relevant data concerning his or her classroom behavior to the school nurse. The nurse tests the student and, if there appears to be a problem, informs the parents of the situation and suggests the proper course of action to alleviate the problem. In some cases, the parents have an option as to whether or not to seek medical help for their child. In many other cases (for example, if the student has a contagious illness), the parents have no option; they must obtain medical help or their child cannot return to school. Teachers do not diagnose or treat health problems. School nurses do not prescribe eyeglasses or hearing aids.

The procedures for identifying, screening, and referring students who may have a drug-related problem are much the same. For example, a math teacher becomes concerned that a student who has repeatedly been late for first-hour math class and has shown a precipitous drop in academic performance may be in trouble with alcohol or other drugs. Her first step would be to clarify the situation with the student by telling him that his performance had clearly deteriorated. The teacher would listen to any explanation the student might offer, but if his work did not improve, her next step would be to refer him and specific data about his behavior to the core team members in charge of preliminary assessment.

Core team members would then gather additional information about the student and screen him for possible drug problems. In some schools, approved data-collection forms would be sent to each of the student's teachers. In other schools, handwritten comments would be submitted or short conferences held between concerned teachers and a core team member. If additional testing and/or treatment seems warranted, the core team would contact the student's parents and recommend that the student be referred to outside services.

Like teachers and school nurses confronting a possible health problem, core team members do not attempt to diagnose or treat drug-related problems. After obtaining parental consent, they must refer students with serious problems to professionals outside the school. In cases of physical and/or sexual abuse by parents, parental permission for a child's referral to a social service agency is not required. In most states, laws mandate that even suspected cases of such abuse be reported immediately to the designated agency.

Need for clear-cut policies and procedures

The basic dynamics of identification and referral are quite simple, but it takes clear-cut policies and procedures to make this program component work. The need for such policies and procedures is especially important if, in the past, the school administration has dealt erratically with drug problems—for example, expelling some students because they are "bad apples" while ignoring others because their parents are influential in the community—or has failed to stand behind teachers who confront drug users. School staff members must be convinced that, in the future, drug-related problems will be handled with consistency and evenhanded concern. Without such assurance, they may be reluctant to make referrals to the core team.

Functions of school drug policies. In general, the very act of establishing school policies on student drug and alcohol use unites the school and the community in work on a common task. Moreover, such policies serve the following specific functions:

- *Acknowledgment of the problem of drug use.* By their very

existence, school drug policies break the no-talk rule and define drug use as a problem that warrants attention.
- *Expression of concern.* Policies testify that top school administrators, community leaders, and the community in general are interested and involved in solving the problem.
- *Assurance of consistent quality of service.* Policies bring uniformity to the school's approach to the problem. Although many principals presume that students would rather not have a policy and would prefer that drug problems were handled on a case-by-case basis, this is not true. Students as well as their families and other concerned persons want to know that the school administration intends to handle student drug problems fairly and consistently.
- *Permission to act.* Policies not only mandate specific activities but also allow for innovation. For some staff members, policies lend support to what they are already doing or want to do; for others, they constitute a kick in the pants.

De facto policy. Every school has a de facto policy on alcohol and drug use. It may consist of either denying the problem except in the case of hard-core delinquents or attempting to drive drug use off the school grounds by surveillance, arrests, and expulsions. The policy of denial obviously is useless because it accomplishes nothing. The policy of punishment is only sporadically successful and is always applied inconsistently. Even if the administration tries to be fair, albeit extremely tough, the punitive approach identifies only those students who are not sophisticated enough to avoid being caught.

Whatever the nature of a school's de facto policy on drug use, it should be assessed on its own merits and in terms of its impact on the early-intervention program. The same is true of every other school policy and procedure. For example, the rules on home-bound instruction and credit for assignments completed outside the classroom will be relevant for students referred for inpatient treatment. Thus, program staff members must know about them and lobby to change them if they adversely affect the program.

Effective policies positively influence the early-intervention processes of identification of problems and initial action taken to resolve them. In general, these two processes should be standardized so that teachers won't waste time pondering before they take action. When policies and procedures have been drafted correctly, teachers know they don't have to offer individual counseling to each student with a problem, don't have to determine whether a problem is really serious enough to warrant a referral outside the school (in-school referral is cost-free and does not disrupt a student's life to any great extent), and don't have to decide to whom the referral should be made. Thus, when a teacher observes drug use or is concerned about a student who may have a drug problem, he or she has less room in which to vacillate before taking initial action. The decisions of when to use discretion and when to be flexible are transferred from teachers, who are already concerned about a multitude of academic issues with a great number of students, to early-intervention program staff

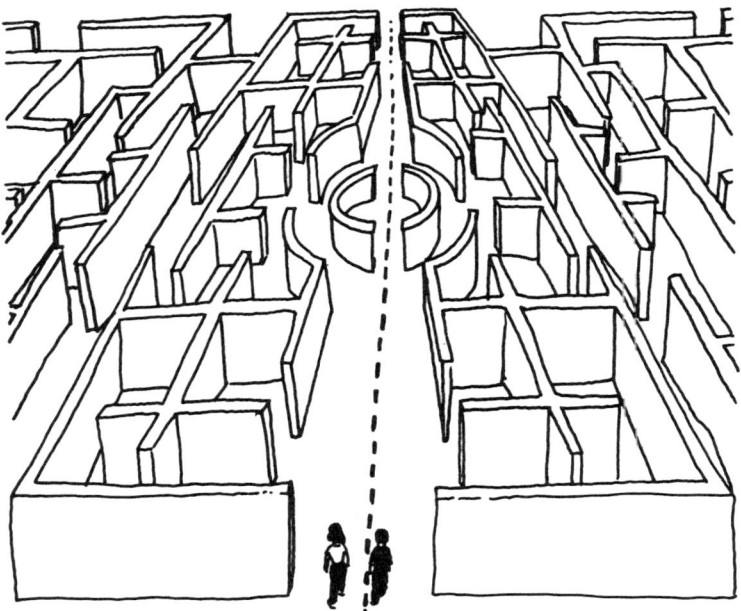

Given effective policies and procedures, school staff members do not waste time pondering over what action to take with troubled students.

members, who are trained to determine whether further action is necessary.

Policy and procedure statements. The format of policy and procedure statements on drug problems should be similar to that of school district documents on other issues. The basic elements of school policy and procedure statements on early intervention for drug problems are as follows:

- a description of the use of alcohol and other drugs by students, family drug problems, general behavioral and emotional problems, and the school's investment in these issues;
- an explanation of the way in which responsibility is to be shared by school staff members and the community at large;
- early-intervention program goals: awareness and education, identification and referral, continuum of counseling and treatment services, and support groups and activities to help students refrain from using drugs;
- personnel specifications: who is needed to do what to make the program work; and
- an acknowledgment of the different qualities and degrees of drug involvement and a delineation of corresponding procedures:
  a. legal issues and disciplinary procedures for:
     (1) possession or intoxication on the school grounds and at school-sanctioned activities,
     (2) selling on the school grounds and at school-sanctioned activities, and
     (3) destructive behavior related to intoxication;
  b. procedures for students suspected of having a drug problem because of a drop in academic performance or an increase in behavioral problems;
  c. procedures for students who voluntarily seek help for personal and/or drug-related problems;
  d. procedures for students referred to treatment, for example, guidelines for sharing confidential information with treatment center staff and giving academic credit for treatment experiences; and
  e. procedures for students whose performance is hampered by drug problems in their families.

Practical identification and referral procedures

Students with drug problems can come to light in any number of ways. However, the dynamics of identification and referral can best be illustrated by considering three of the most common ways: (1) breaking public laws and school rules against drug possession, sale, and intoxication; (2) failing academically, skipping school, or not participating in classes; and (3) voluntarily requesting help.

How to handle infractions. Students caught drinking or using some other drug on the school grounds are usually sent to the school nurse, who decides whether immediate medical treatment is necessary. If a student is under the influence of a drug, the parents are summoned to take him or her home and a disciplinary conference is scheduled (for the next day, if possible). At this conference, the assistant principal imposes a short- or long-term suspension, depending on the seriousness of the infraction.

In schools without drug programs, the process usually ends here. Past experience has shown, however, that discipline alone is a woefully crude tool for dealing with student drug problems. While a suspension may indeed be enough to shake up a student who is not deeply involved with drugs, it may have the opposite effect on a student who is deeply involved with drugs or a student whose family life is so painful that drug use will continue to be his or her main solace, despite the threat of further disciplinary ation. For such students, suspensions may simply alienate them from all authority figures. What's more, they are given more unstructured time in which to use drugs freely.

In schools with an early-intervention program, the disciplinary process is just a beginning, not an end in itself. To be effective, discipline must be meted out consistently. Thus, if an assistant principal imposes a three-day suspension on one student for possessing acohol or other drugs on school grounds, he or she must do the same for every other student caught committing the same infraction. Furthermore, in-school suspension, that is, keeping a student in school but isolated from the general school population, is preferable to sending him or her out on the streets for several days. If policymakers want the option of foregoing disciplinary consequences in certain cases, they must spell out the exceptions and make them known to students and staff alike. Such consistency and openness relay two important messages. First, the school staff won't look the other way to avoid problems. Second, all infractions will be taken seriously.

While disciplinary options are still under consideration or after appropriate discipline has been meted out, the core team begins to gather information about the student as part of a preliminary assessment. Was this student just flaunting his first marijuana joint to gain prestige from his peers, or is he always so stoned that he neither knew nor cared that everyone could see the joint? Does this appear to be the first time that he has ever engaged in such behavior, or does he or others report that this is simply one incident in a long history of drug use? The core team may not need to gather very much information if the student is a notorious drug user and all of his teachers are amazed that he wasn't caught sooner. If this is the case, his parents are called in, evidence of their son's drug problem is presented to them, and a referral to a treatment center may be more or less instantaneous. If the parents refuse to take any rehabilitative action, the school simply follows normal disciplinary procedures fully and to the letter. If the problem of neglect or abuse by parents comes to light and the child is deemed to be in clear danger if rehabilitative action is not taken, the school contacts the appropriate social service agency.

If the case is less clear-cut, however, the core team gathers information from three sources: teachers, parents, and the student. It is the responsibility of the core team to give some guidance both to teachers and to parents as to how to gather specific, useful information. Usually this process involves little investigation on the part of teachers or parents; often it is simply a matter of their reflecting on and writing down recent, specific instances in which the student or any of his associates alluded to drug use or the student was clearly intoxicated or extremely uncooperative and unwilling to communicate. A single piece of data from any one source rarely provides the impetus for taking effective action; data collected from a variety of sources are more likely to be influential.

Discipline alone is a woefully crude tool for dealing with student drug problems.

Once all the information has been gathered, the preliminary assessment counselor or the core team decides whether the data point to a serious drug, personal, or family problem. If so, the parents are called in and a referral to an outside agency is made. If evidence is lacking or if the data paint a fuzzy picture, the student may then be suspended or referred to an insight group. Other options include assigning him to an ongoing support group in the school or continuing to monitor the situation for review at a later date.

How to handle possible drug-related academic problems. Some students may come to the staff's attention because of difficulties with schoolwork, attendance, or class participation. If their performance shows that they simply are not learning the assigned material and if, when questioned about it, they do not seem to care, teachers should proceed with the usual options and consequences that accompany academic failure. If these attempts do not result in any improvement, a teacher may then refer a student to the core team for a preliminary assessment. If the student's parents have not yet been made aware of the problem, they are informed at this point.

The early-intervention program depends, then, upon the alertness and responsiveness of school staff members. As I've already stated, teachers are *not* expected to become alcohol/drug abuse experts; they *are* expected to pursue problems related to academic performance. Although they can exercise discretion in matters related to the teaching of their particular discipline, they *cannot* decide that a student is simply not worth their effort and so will not be expected to perform. To make the early-intervention process work, teachers must pursue every performance problem until it is resolved or until it is referred to an appropriate school resource, including a member of the core team.

It is essential that academic failure not automatically be presumed to be the result of drug use. Only after it has been determined that learning disabilities or other issues are not the cause of a student's academic failure should the student be referred to the early-intervention program.

A word of caution is needed here concerning students referred outside the school for an in-depth assessment. The early-intervention program staff must make certain that these students are sent to an assessment service that is not biased toward diagnosing chemical dependency or any other favored behavioral or psychiatric condition. A reliable, unbiased assessment agency in the community can be of tremendous help to schools that are implementing early-intervention programs.

How to handle self-referrals. By the second or third year of a school-based program, more and more students with drug and other personal problems will be coming in to talk about their experiences and their fears for themselves and for their friends. They will seek advice, they will want someone to know what's going on, and they will ask for help. At this point, the

program will have shifted gears. It will truly be an
early-intervention program. The entire problem won't be licked
in just two or three years, but the school environment will have
changed enough so that individual students will receive help
sooner than they would have in the past.

The fact that students will come out into the open about
their drug use surprises many people, especially those who
think that only law-and-order policies do the job. The truth is,
kids with drug problems will come forward voluntarily *if*
disciplinary actions for infractions are applied consistently and
if the awareness and education presentations have informed
and convinced people that something can be done about drug
problems.

Insight groups

One method of screening and intervention being used by more
and more schools is what we at Community Intervention, Inc.,
call an insight group: a time-limited, structured series of
didactic presentations, group discussions, and confrontations
regarding the participants' use of chemicals. Typically, an
insight group is made up of 9 to 12 students who have been
identified or have identified themselves as having some
drug-related problems. While formats can vary, a typical
insight group meets for nine 50-minute sessions per cycle; each
cycle lasts three weeks, with three group sessions held per
week. This tight format allows sessions to be readily integrated
into the school day. Each session consists of about 20 minutes
of formal presentation and 30 minutes of discussion, role
playing, or some other form of interaction.

Students referred to an insight group (sometimes called an
insight class) take part in an easily understood process in
which staff facilitators specify expectations for behavior, set
group goals, and provide tools to help participants perform a
variety of learning activities. Class schedules, procedures for
placement in the group, parent and student contract forms,
basic information on drug issues, and a student workbook are
all provided by the facilitators. Usually the workbook consists
of material derived from a variety of sources and modified
when necessary.

In an insight group, anxieties are diminished because participants know what to expect and manipulation is minimized because the structured format leaves little room for maneuvering. During the nine sessions, students discuss why they were referred to the insight group, fill out questionnaires about their drug use, learn about the range and progression of drug use problems, and identify the roles that their feelings and defenses play in their use of alcohol or other drugs. They also are confronted, either by the facilitators or by the other participants, about their own drug use.

After a student has completed a cycle, he or she meets with a member of the core team to review what he or she has learned and to explore the possible need for further action. Parents are usually involved in this review.

COUNSELING AND TREATMENT

Just as school counselors and teachers are not expected to become alcohol/drug abuse counselors, schools are not expected to become treatment centers. Nonetheless, schools do have an important role to play in ensuring that students and their families have access to an adequate continuum of counseling and treatment services, including but not limited to the following:

- in-depth assessment and referral services;
- family and individual counseling;
- outpatient treatment for drug and alcohol problems;
- inpatient treatment for drug and alcohol problems; and
- long-term residential treatment.

The schools' role is to establish close communication with counseling and treatment agencies and to staunchly support the creation of needed services if they do not already exist in the community. The data gathered by school staff members can be especially important to professionals in the community who must perform in-depth assessments of students and their families. Close communication is imperative if the school is to provide these professionals with a clear picture of a student's behavior at school and at home. Similarly, if a school and a treatment center are to implement a method by which students can complete their schoolwork while in treatment or provide compatible support services for students who have completed treatment, communication and cooperation between the two systems are absolutely essential.

SUPPORT

Change doesn't come easily to adults recovering from alcoholism or drug addiction, and it comes even harder to recovering adolescents. Adults returning to their workplaces and homes after treatment do not face the same challenges that kids do when they return to school. Adults usually aren't encouraged to drink on the job, but if they are, they can find another job. Furthermore, participation in an evening support group sponsored by Alcoholics Anonymous or by their treatment center often is enough to help adults maintain their sobriety.

In contrast, young people who have been in primary treatment usually must return to the very environment where they first learned to use drugs. They return to find their old friends right where they left them, still smoking a joint or two at the side door before class. "Welcome back!" says one of them. "You didn't turn into a narc, did you? Want a toke? I'm having a hard time this week. Can't make it without a little smoke . . . ."

In this milieu, it doesn't take long before returning students feel the same old anxieties, the same old fears. Suddenly, they are not sure what's "real": the personal, warm, confrontive, "straight" world of the treatment center and all they learned there *or* the drug world they chose for themselves before they went into treatment.

Obviously, if kids are to capitalize on the gains they make in treatment or to refrain from using drugs without treatment, they desperately need the support and help of their families, their friends and peers, and the staff at school.

Schools' role in providing support

In this context, support simply means helping kids who do not want to use chemicals to attain this goal. Since reentry into school constitutes the greatest danger for students completing treatment and just starting to work on living without drugs, schools must act to minimize this danger. One way the school can do this is to have a core team member meet with each student returning from treatment before he or she reenters school to help plan his or her schedule and to discuss particular fears, such as facing drug-using peers again. Such a meeting lets the student know that he or she won't have to go it alone.

Of course, the vast majority of young people identified as drug users in an early-intervention program never need inpatient primary treatment. Many stop using after simple parental/school intervention. Others need the support of non-drug-using peers, informally or in a structured group, and some succeed in outpatient treatment. Whatever the particular circumstance, a school staff member should maintain close ties with family members, probation officers, social workers, and any other person concerned about a student who is trying to stay off drugs.

Setting up student support groups is perhaps the best way for schools to help students during the first six months or year of their struggle to stay off alcohol or other drugs. To be effective, these groups should meet during the school day at least once a week. Whenever possible, they should be led by a core team member or other trained school staff member and cofacilitated by a community volunteer. Students who want to be involved in a support group are often asked to sign a contract stating that they will stay off drugs and fulfill their obligations and responsibilities in school. Some students may also be asked to make a formal commitment to continue working on important personal issues.

The objectives of student support groups are to—

- encourage group members to initiate friendships with kids who do not use drugs;
- offer support specifically for abstaining from the use of mood-altering chemicals;
- help group members achieve personal goals;
- confront group members about behavioral patterns that frequently precede a return to drug use; and

Young people who return to school after chemical dependency treatment face intense peer pressure to start using again.

- provide a trusting, open, feelings-oriented environment in which group members can nurture their own and one another's growth.

To be sure, these objectives are limited, but the school time allotted for such groups is also, by necessity, limited. Although school-based support groups are much less intensive than aftercare groups sponsored by treatment centers, they *are* in the school, where they are so urgently needed.

The subject of facilitating student support groups is far too broad for me to address here. I would, however, like to offer three guidelines that can help neophyte facilitators avoid a great deal of difficulty when they begin to work with students. First, facilitators of support groups should not provide ongoing counseling to students who have emotional, family, or sexual problems. Such counseling falls within the domain of the network of mental health centers and social service agencies. Second, there are advantages to assigning students who have gone to treatment and those who have not to separate support groups. Often, a treatment center has its own idiosyncratic language and philosophy. Those who have not been through treatment are often uncomfortable with the terms employed by those who have and are threatened by the open communication and confrontation that treatment graduates manifest. Third, it is especially important not to mix the function of an insight group with that of a support group. Kids who are trying to refrain from drug use need all the positive support they can get; they should not be burdened with peers who may still be hostile to the idea of nonuse.

Schools interested in taking an intervention-to-prevention approach to the drug problem should not ignore those students who have never used chemicals. They need support, too. To provide this support, some school districts now offer short-term support groups to nonusers considered to be at risk for first-time drug use—for example, students who have just moved from another school or district and students whose parents are in the process of divorce. In addition to these support groups, school publications, convocations, rallies, and other activities can serve as vehicles by which staff and students can recognize and support those students who have never used drugs. All these measures can help to create an environment in which all nonusers gain some status and receive approval for abstaining from drug use.

Support for children of alcoholics

Schools can offer a tremendous service to the community by making support services available to the children of alcoholics. No other system in the community—and this includes treatment centers for adult alcoholics—has a greater opportunity to reach this very needy group of young people. Many school-based programs currently offer services to the children of alcoholics and a number of methods, including concerned persons groups, are clearly having positive effects. Appendix A lists two books that provide valuable information about the children of alcoholics.

For those who work with these children in a group or individually, in a formal therapeutic setting or even on an informal basis, the following guidelines can be helpful:

- *Let them know that they are not alone.* Assure them that others share their experiences and understand their feelings.
- *Validate their experiences.* Help them sort out their confusion and explain that although they may feel "crazy," they aren't. They are reacting to parents who downplay or ignore the severity of their own problems, deny that certain events ever took place, and behave inconsistently.
- *Help them gain some perspective on how their parent's alcoholism has affected them.* It has often been said that children from alcoholic families fall into predictable, unhealthy patterns of behavior as a reaction to this problem. Some become overly responsible to compensate for the irresponsibility of a parent, others act out constantly to get attention from an otherwise inattentive parent, and so forth. Groups for children of alcoholics can help them to identify and consider ways of changing their patterns of behavior.
- *Absolve them of blame.* Convince them of the fact that their mother's or father's drinking is not their fault and that they can't control it.
- *Help them separate the parent from the drunken behavior.* Make it clear that their parent's drinking is not a sign that their mother or father does not love them. Ask them to remember,

if they can, what it was like at home before their parent started drinking heavily.
- *Offer them hope.* Let them know that alcoholism is a disease from which their parent can recover.
- *Urge them to take care of themselves.* Encourage them to do positive things for themselves and stop any of their own behavior that enables their mother or father to continue drinking. Sometimes, making a contract with these children helps them achieve their goals.
- *Provide them with a safe outlet for dealing with their anger.* Help them deal with their anger at both the alcoholic parent and the nonalcoholic parent (who has not protected them or made things better).
- *Explain their risks related to chemical dependency.* Make them aware that they are at high risk of becoming chemically dependent or of marrying a chemically dependent person. Children of alcoholics about to leave home tend to believe that their troubles will soon be over. They need to know that they are more likely to encounter certain problems than children raised in families in which alcoholism is not an issue. This has to be handled very judiciously. Be careful not to use the label "child of an alcoholic" as though that particular aspect of their life totally defines their present identity and future actions. Nonetheless, it is clear that, for a variety of reasons, the children of alcoholics are at high risk of becoming chemically dependent and, at the proper time and in the proper way, should be made aware of that fact.
- *Build their self-esteem.* Help raise the self-esteem of these children in whatever way possible. Simply having an adult listen closely to them can boost the self-esteem of many of these children.

SUMMARY OF SCHOOL-BASED PROGRAMMING

In this and previous chapters, we've covered the internal organization as well as the primary functions of a school-based early-intervention program. The core team and program coordinator, taking most of the responsibility for designing and implementing the program within the school, work with the guidance of an advisory board of interested citizens from the community to implement the following four components of programming:

- *Awareness and education.* Targeted first at adults and then at students, this component addresses the range and progression of drug use problems, the conspiracy of silence that generally envelops drug and alcohol use and abuse, the various ways in which well-meaning adults inadvertently enable young people to continue using drugs, and the initial action steps to take once a problem has been identified.
- *Identification and referral.* Schools are in an excellent position to identify students with drug or other personal problems and to gather relevant data that can be used in confronting the problem and determining the best way to help each student.
- *Counseling and treatment.* Although schools can offer some simple, straightforward advice to students and parents about the need for taking further action on a drug or other personal problem, the social service providers in the community have the primary responsibility for providing direct assistance to those in need of more help than the schools can offer. Schools can play a very important role in the assessment process by passing on pertinent information concerning a student's behavior at school. Schools can also stay in close contact with service providers (when parents and students sign appropriate release-of-confidential-information forms) in order to coordinate the school's support services and class schedules with counseling and treatment services provided by treatment centers and other agencies in the community.
- *Support.* Schools have a major role to play in helping those students who wish to refrain from drug use to do so. Student support groups and activities are congruent both with the school's role regarding drug problems and with the school's ability to provide such support.

PROGRAM EVALUATION

Once the school board has approved the task force's program proposal and given the appropriate financial and organizational backing, it is possible to make the school-based early-intervention program functional within three to five months. Thus, if the program is approved during the winter or early spring, it can be in operation by the time school opens again in the fall.

Regardless of when the program starts, it should be allowed a full two years to prove its worth. Undoubtedly, the simple, straightforward, and consistent approach to drug problems suggested here will pay immediate dividends both to the school and to the community. However, not until a program has won the trust and support of school staff members, parents, and students will the real benefit of the early-intervention approach become evident. When most of the referrals to the program come from students and parents rather than from disciplinary actions, the program will be in full stride, with intervention occurring *before* students become enmeshed in drug use.

Program evaluation in any social service or educational field can be complex. Don't let the complexities of an in-depth evaluation lead to a postponement of a critical review of the school's early-intervention efforts, however. From the outset, core team and advisory board members can assess, modify, and improve the program. Keep asking such commonsense, relevant questions as:

- Were most of the participants in the first parent drug awareness program from one racial or ethnic group even though the school serves a multiracial/multiethnic district? Should a way be found to attract the attention of other groups before the next program?
- Are more children of alcoholics than expected coming forward? Should extra help or training be sought for core team members and the school staff?
- Have program staff members heard a rumor that teachers aren't making referrals to the core team because they suspect that the administration doesn't really support the program? Should the administration be persuaded to reaffirm its support?
- Is the core team swamped with phone calls from parents asking for specific information about local services? Should a directory of local services be compiled and distributed? Can the advisory board be of help in this regard?

These and hundreds of other questions will assail members of the core team and advisory board soon after the program begins to operate. By keeping track of questions as they arise and making every attempt to answer them as soon as possible, the program staff can rest assured that the program will be finely tuned and working at maximum capability within a relatively short period.

* * * * * * * *

In the preceding chapters, we've looked at the rationale, theory, and practice of mobilizing communities to develop and implement early-intervention programs for young drug users. In the next chapter, I'll relate how adults in Ohio and Montana have employed these concepts to meet the needs of young people.

Part Two

CHAPTER SEVEN
Success in Ohio and Montana

No two communities approach community intervention, community mobilization, and school-based drug programming in quite the same manner. Nor do they find the same route around, through, or over the barriers that can impede progress. Community mobilization as I've described it thus far is really just the bare bones of a story that every community completes in its own way, using its own resources. In this chapter, I'll add some important details by telling the stories of two quite different mobilization efforts. Both stories span several years of multicommunity action. In Ohio, the courageous, decisive action of the superintendents of 41 school districts helped launch their respective communities into mobilizing against adolescent drug use. In Montana, mobilization began with a grass-roots effort on the part of parents who formed a strong liaison with businesspeople and volunteers.

THE OHIO STORY: SUPERINTENDENTS LEAD THE WAY

When the new school year began in the fall of 1979, there was one drug awareness program active in the school districts of suburban Cleveland. Within four years, 62 school districts in the Greater Cleveland area had joined together to offer extensive drug intervention and prevention services to more than 200,000 students. Operating independently but in a cooperative and mutually supportive manner, school-based programs are now available to more than 10% of all the students in Ohio.

A call to action

Many people trace this meteoric rise in alcohol and drug programming back to November 1979, when the Greater Cleveland School Superintendents Association held a well-publicized press conference on the problems caused by alcohol and drug use in the schools. In that press conference, the superintendents described the problem as they saw it, named a subcommittee whose task would be to address the problem within and among the participating districts, and challenged the community at large to join them in their fight against chemical abuse. The press conference has since been referred to as "The Call to Action."

Naming itself Project C.A.R.E. (Chemical Abuse Reduced By Education), the subcommittee hosted two important symposia in February and April 1980. Present at the symposia were school superintendents from all member districts of the Superintendents Association, other school personnel, and representatives from each school's community. Participants at these symposia were encouraged to return to their communities and form "community action teams" to begin the fight against drug and alcohol abuse on the local level. These community action teams—often called Project C.A.R.E. committees or CAT teams—became a major force in the Greater Cleveland area.

Although the unanimous support of members of the Superintendents Association provided a powerful endorsement for innovative action in the schools, the type of programming needed remained unclear. It was then that the Regional Council on Alcoholism made a valuable contribution.

The Regional Council on Alcoholism

From 1974 to 1979, the Region Twelve division of the Regional Council on Alcoholism, which serves the Greater Cleveland area, tried unsuccessfully to influence the schools in its four-county region. Although it made some gains in curriculum development, its efforts to win top-level administrative support proved unsuccessful. When the Regional Council shifted its emphasis from curriculum development to awareness and education events as part of early-intervention programming for the schools, the situation rapidly improved.

In April 1980, the Regional Council sponsored the first early-intervention workshop ever held in the Greater Cleveland area, a six-day session on "Alcohol and Drugs: Working With Adolescents and Schools" conducted by Community Intervention, Inc., of Minneapolis. The workshop had a very positive impact on the participants, many of whom went on to develop unique and effective programs in the schools and social service agencies in their communities. These participants also encouraged others to attend training workshops and become involved in drug and alcohol abuse programs.

Communitywide involvement

With the Superintendents Association and the Regional Council providing a context for change and a model for community mobilization, other groups joined their ranks. In 1981, six school districts followed the Regional Council's lead and sponsored ten more workshops in the Greater Cleveland area. By the end of 1981, more than 900 people had been trained in intensive weeklong sessions and more than 25,000 adults and 27,000 students had participated in a variety of shorter awareness events sponsored by Project C.A.R.E.

In addition, the community action teams were having remarkable success in developing a broad base of support. By the winter of 1982, about half of the 1,137 team members were school employees and the rest were parents, representatives from municipal governments, churches, community service organizations, and members of various professional groups. Such support allowed the trained school personnel (referred to in most districts as core teams) to work on everything from curriculum development and in-school abstinence support groups to community-based self-help groups for families with chemically dependent children. By late 1982, several community action teams were also lobbying to convince state legislators and social service providers of the need for additional services for young people with drug problems.

Creation of services

As the level of awareness of alcohol and drug problems increased in the Greater Cleveland area, so too did the rate of identification of chemically dependent and substance-abusing young people. For several years, United Methodist Alcohol Counseling Center (UMACC) had been offering quality assessment and intervention services and urging other agencies to create similar services or expand existing services to include adolescents. It now drew new support for its plea from the Regional Council's Youth Planning Committee and numerous Project C.A.R.E. committees. Public awareness of the growing number of young people who needed help led to the development of a far wider range of assessment, intervention, primary treatment, and aftercare services than had previously existed.

Statewide action

The Greater Akron area was quick to follow suit. By June 1981, representatives from 24 school districts and their respective communities had organized under the name "Community Intervention Against Adolescent Drug/Alcohol Abuse Committee." This committee sponsored the first area symposium, which was held at the University of Akron. Staff members of the Region Ten division of the Regional Council on Alcoholism were helping the committee plan a Community Intervention, Inc., workshop for the schools in Region Ten's five-county district. They were duplicating what others had done in Greater Cleveland. School staff members and community representatives were being selected for the first Akron-Summit County area workshop to be held in August 1981. Akron area schools had already contacted the suburban Cleveland school districts, which by then were evaluating the effectiveness of their new programs. Cooperation was extensive; networking was expansive; school districts were finding new reasons to interact with one another.

The Region Ten Council and the committee cosponsored the first Community Intervention, Inc., workshop in August 1981. Seventy eager participants left training prepared to begin the task of early-intervention program development for students in the Greater Akron area. Since that workshop, 1,049 individuals have been trained in 16 workshops cosponsored by the school districts and the Region Ten Council.

During this same period, several adult treatment facilities in the Greater Akron area established chemical dependency units for adolescents or expanded their existing programs to include adolescent treatment. In addition, community action teams sent participants to locally conducted awareness and education programs, the University of Akron granted for-credit status to Community Intervention, Inc., workshops, and six chapters of Families Anonymous were established in the Akron-Canton area.

Among the participants at the first Akron workshop were staff members from the Northeastern Ohio Regional Council on Alcoholism (Region Eleven), which serves the Greater Youngstown area. These representatives returned enthused about the successes in Cleveland and Akron. They found it a simple matter to sell the same idea to the schools and communities in Greater Youngstown.

Basically, mobilization efforts in Youngstown followed the pattern developed in Cleveland and Akron. Representatives from area schools and communities were sent to training and returned with stories about the success of other school districts. They were able to point to their counterparts in other sections of northeastern Ohio who were effectively dealing with adolescent alcohol and drug problems in their schools and communities. Success breeds success, and in October 1981, the Region Eleven Council and the Youngstown public school system cosponsored the first area Community Intervention, Inc., workshop. They have since cosponsored six additional workshops, networking with schools throughout northern Ohio and western Pennsylvania.

Among the people trained in the Greater Youngstown area were representatives from local mental health agencies. As a result, these service providers have instituted assessment and intervention services to complement school-based programs and referrals. Selected staff members from a variety of agencies have been trained by Community Intervention, Inc., and the network of schools, agencies, and communities is growing rapidly. Other sections of Ohio are examining the successes of these northeastern Ohio pioneers, while expansion of training, school-based programming, and counseling and treatment services continues throughout Greater Cleveland, Akron, and Youngstown.

DYNAMICS OF THE OHIO STORY

Change in the Greater Cleveland area (and later in Akron and Youngstown) can be attributed to the many unique contributions of hundreds of creative, enthusiastic individuals. The major contribution, however, came from the interaction of the following groups:

- *Greater Cleveland School Superintendents Association.* The Superintendents Association provided a context for change by identifying the problem, making a public commitment to finding solutions, and offering a means of planning in the form of Project C.A.R.E. and the community action teams.
- *Regional Council on Alcoholism.* Various divisions of the Regional Council not only provided their expertise in the area of alcohol abuse but also helped to bring together school staff members, social service professionals, and outside consultants, whose combined efforts gave direction to the communities working for change.
- *Community Intervention, Inc.* This organization provided training in early-intervention techniques. Its model for drug programming proved acceptable to all groups and helped people become effective agents of change.

Let's take a closer look at the dynamics of the Ohio story. Some may or may not be applicable in other communities.

Public, united, top-level support

The superintendents of all suburban Cleveland school districts willingly and publicly acknowledged, "We all have a problem in our districts."

Their public statement was a courageous, irrevocable commitment to action. It mobilized many people whose awareness and concern were limited and strongly endorsed the efforts of those individuals already working for change.

By presenting a united front, the superintendents left no room for doubt that adolescent drug use was a pervasive problem in all school districts. Thus, no single school could be faulted for being more problem-ridden than another. Blaming was minimized and the need for cooperation emphasized. By sticking together, the superintendents provided a "protective umbrella" under which real solutions could be explored.

A word of caution: High-powered publicity techniques must be used judiciously. For example, if a group of disgruntled teachers had called a press conference without the cooperation of the school superintendents, some action may have been taken, but distrust and suspicion on the part of top-level administrators could have permanently plagued the project.

Shared responsibility

The school superintendents did not take full responsibility for causing the problem or for solving it.

As one school superintendent stated, "Chemical use in the schools is not just a school problem. It definitely is a problem in the schools because the kids who are using drugs cannot function, but it is also a community problem. People tend to blame the schools for the problem. However, this problem is brought into the schools from the outside world, the adult world, and we need the adult world to solve it."

Start-up funds from an outside source

The Martha Holden Jennings Foundation in Cleveland granted $6,000 to Project C.A.R.E. to conduct the first symposium.

Without the $6,000 grant, the symposium might have been delayed for weeks or even months while each school district independently decided whether or not it could free a minute portion of its budget to support this crucial initial effort. Such a delay could have been a major setback for the entire process of community mobilization. As it turned out, however, the search for start-up funds from an outside source yielded more than money. It also challenged the schools to define and articulate the overall need for adolescent drug programs and to demonstrate their willingness and ability to supply the staff, time, and commitment needed to further their own cause.

Action, not just awareness

The Project C.A.R.E. symposium was divided into two sessions. In the morning, the audience listened to speakers who explained the problem and the concept of community action. In the afternoon, audience members met in small groups to plan specific agendas for their own communities.

The field of drug and alcohol abuse abounds with entertaining speakers who can come to communities and rouse audiences with their verbal pyrotechnics. However, unless these speakers also offer practical ideas as to how audience members can work to solve the problem, little is accomplished. The Project C.A.R.E. effort was oriented toward community action from the beginning, and this approach paid off in the end.

Temporary use of out-of-state services

The absence of chemical dependency units for adolescents in the Greater Cleveland area meant that young drug abusers had to be sent to Louisiana or Minnesota for inpatient treatment.

Generally, treatment services are not created until the need for them has been demonstrated. School personnel and community action teams knew that the number of adolescents identified as being chemically dependent would steadily increase. Consequently, they immediately began pushing to have treatment centers established in the Greater Cleveland area. In the meantime, chemically dependent adolescents were sent to out-of-state treatment centers. Although this filled the gap, it is not a practical long-term solution.

Judicious use of consultants

Community Intervention, Inc., has provided consultants and ongoing training services to most school districts throughout northeastern Ohio. Although their input has been considerable, these consultants have not assumed positions of permanent leadership. Leadership should come from the inside, with consultation and training being provided from the outside.

In the early stages of community mobilization and program development, people often find it difficult to know when to bring in outside consultants and trainers and when to work independently. This issue eventually resolves itself as people gain experience working in their own systems and communities, begin to trust one another's skills and judgments, accept their collective strengths and limitations, and learn that some tasks can be accomplished only with outside help.

Large-scale training effort

More than 3,000 people in northeastern Ohio had been trained by Community Intervention, Inc., by March 1984.

A community can benefit by sending two or three individuals to a training workshop because they will return with new ideas and techniques. However, if the community wants to make extensive changes, it must invest in a large-scale training effort. In the Greater Cleveland area, such training provided a strong local base of shared concepts and enthusiasm. Granted, all the participants may not have agreed with everything they learned during training, but they now work within a mutually understood framework that allows them to argue, compromise, and plan effectively.

THE MONTANA STORY: PARENTS ORGANIZE A GRASS-ROOTS MOVEMENT

Until 1980, most communities in Montana had been striving to do something about their own adolescent alcohol and drug problems, but each community was merely coping in isolation. A welter of small programs had sprung up over the years, but most had faltered because of a lack of community support. None of the few treatment centers in the state dealt specifically with adolescent chemical abusers. School-based programs for young people and their families did not exist.

Pressure from parents

By mid-1980, however, the members of a self-help group for parents of adolescent drug abusers in the Billings area were beginning to see the futility of dealing with the adolescent drug problem on a case-by-case basis and were taking the first steps toward developing a communitywide action plan. They had had some success in helping chemically dependent adolescents by intervening with their parents and using out-of-state treatment services. However, they were stymied in their efforts to get local professionals—educators, psychologists, social workers, physicians, psychiatrists, and others—to understand the problem of adolescent drug abuse and to see the need for counseling and treatment services in the Billings area. When they approached the schools to solicit their assistance in establishing some type of program, any type of program, to help students who had drug problems, they were turned down flat.

It soon became obvious to them that if early-intervention, primary treatment, and aftercare programs were ever to be established in the Billings area, community education and training were needed to convince people of the need for such programs and to teach them the basic steps in establishing them. There was so little interest in the problem, however, that raising the minimal funds needed to initiate the education and training process was proving to be extremely difficult. It was at this point that the business community, led by Wendy's Old Fashioned Hamburgers of Montana, stepped in.

The business connection

The people at Wendy's are committed to and interested in the health and welfare of their many teenage employees. The Billings parents group hoped to capitalize on this commitment and interest. Sensing that the time was right, the group asked Sam McDonald, chairman of the board of Wendy's of Montana, for the funds needed to send 15 people to a training workshop offered by Community Intervention, Inc., in Minneapolis. When he agreed to sponsor the training venture, the first important liaison between parents and the business community was formed.

This liaison has proved to be a very powerful factor in the growth of alcohol and drug education, training, and program development in Montana. By September 1980, the parents and professionals who had attended the Minneapolis workshop had succeeded in raising the funds and the awareness needed to have Community Intervention, Inc., conduct a training workshop in Billings. Like the Minneapolis training event, the Billings workshop was funded primarily by Wendy's, although many other groups made important donations.

Proliferation of training workshops

Sixty-five people attended the first Billings workshop in June 1980. A number of these participants eventually made significant contributions to the growth and development of services elsewhere in Montana.

Word about the first workshop spread rapidly, and in August 1981, the second workshop was held. By the close of 1981, a total of 330 Montanans had been trained in intensive, one-week, action-oriented workshops. By December 1982, trainees numbered 800 and by December 1983, a total of 1,300 people had been trained. From the forested mountains of Kalispell in the west to the windblown plains of Glendive 500 miles to the east, every major community in Montana, including Billings, Bozeman, Helena, Butte, Missoula, Great Falls, Cut Bank, Lewistown, and Sidney, had sponsored at least one weeklong workshop by the end of 1983.

Development of school-based programs

Before 1980, some Montana schools had offered drug education programs, but most had relied on a hard-line disciplinary approach, trying to "scare 'em straight." The assistant superintendent of the Great Falls public school system has said, "For years I patted myself on the back for how efficiently we kicked kids out of school. But we weren't doing a thing about the real problem. We still have rules and discipline, but now we can offer alternatives as well."

By the close of 1983, all class-AA schools, most class-A schools, and the schools in many smaller districts in Montana had set up early-intervention programs. The Great Falls CA/RE (Chemical Abuse/Responsive Education) program is representative of these programs. As part of the CA/RE program, trained school staff members and community volunteers cofacilitate a variety of support groups:

- Insight groups, which help those students caught using or possessing drugs to evaluate their own use, often serve as an alternative to suspension, expulsion, or court fines.
- Concerned persons groups offer support for students concerned about someone else's drug or alcohol use.
- Abstinence support groups help students who have decided to abstain from chemical use.
- Aftercare support groups assist students returning from treatment.
- Parent support groups meet weekly to allow parents to share concerns and information about adolescent drug use.
- Awareness groups provide junior high students with a source of information about alcohol and drug use, abuse, and dependency.

Since 1981, when the Great Falls CA/RE program was established, these support groups have become increasingly effective. In the 1982-1983 school year, a total of 761 students participated in groups. Of the 201 students who went through insight groups, 72 were referred to outside agencies for an in-depth assessment; 41 of the 72 underwent treatment. Prior to the CA/RE program, most of these 201 students would have been suspended or expelled.

Administrators' participation in training

Strong administrative support is the mainstay of the school-based program in Great Falls, as it is in Glendive, Helena, Cut Bank, Kalispell, and other Montana communities. School administrators determine whether or not all core team members have the same hour free for meetings each day, whether or not relationships between the school staff and the community are facilitated, and most important, whether or not the program is implemented.

In Montana, school administrators have been supportive

from the outset. In large part, this stems from the fact that so many of them have been through training. In Great Falls, for example, all high school, junior high, and elementary school principals and vice-principals have participated in training workshops. They were joined by the deans of students, counselors, and other school staff members.

Because of this training, many administrators have become members, or leaders, of core teams, giving the team authority in the eyes of students, parents, and other staff members. Their involvement eases the implementation of policy and procedure changes and has the invaluable side effect of improving staff/administration communication. It also is personally gratifying. As a vice-principal of a senior high school stated, "When you work and sweat, intervene, take risks, and still end up losing a kid, it's a lot different than when you just scratch a note saying 'Good-bye, kid.' There's a lot of stress in this commitment, but now I wouldn't do it any other way."

Volunteer support

"It would be suicidal for us to try to accomplish this programming without volunteers," said one teacher who serves as a core team leader. "It's a good thing they keep coming forward after every parent and community drug awareness program." He was referring to the legions of volunteers who have supported school and community programs in Great Falls during three years of intensive programming efforts.

In Bozeman, volunteers spearheaded the fund-raising campaign that brought a training workshop to town and thus launched a communitywide programming effort. In the beginning, a few concerned parents took it upon themselves to raise the money needed to finance the workshop. As they went door to door requesting funds from businesses, the people they approached began to share their concern. Within just a few months, numerous others had joined their cause and they raised $15,000.

In Great Falls, the Junior League, an organization that promotes volunteerism among women, has played a significant role in almost every phase of programming. Indeed, Junior Leaguers were among the first Great Falls residents to recognize the need for a communitywide solution and backed up that recognition by participating in training workshops. In addition, the League's organizational expertise and connections throughout the community have been helpful in fund raising, in hosting training workshops, and in compiling and publishing an informational handbook for parents.

Changes in juvenile court systems

The various juvenile court systems in Montana have begun to work with communities to ensure that adolescents in trouble with the law because of drug-related offenses receive the attention their problems deserve. At one time, existing laws gave the courts just three choices in dealing with such adolescents: a fine, referral to protective services, or a sentence to be served in a jail for adults. Recently, many individuals working in the juvenile court systems have taken the lead in creating other alternatives.

In turn, each community has devised its own variations based upon available services and the degree of cooperation afforded by city and county agencies. In Kalispell, for example, when a youth is picked up by police for a first-time DUI offense, he or she is sent to a drug education class. For a second offense, he or she joins an orange-vested work crew in cleaning up local roadsides. A third offense calls for mandatory assessment and, more than likely, treatment for an alcohol or drug problem. In Glendive, a student caught on a drug-related offense is referred to the school-based awareness and education class. If he or she doesn't perform well there, he or she is referred to Alcohol and Drug Services for further assessment. In Great Falls, youths picked up for possession or a DUI offense during the summer are referred to summer insight groups run by community volunteers in close association with the school-based program.

Special training a priority for helping professionals

Social service professionals in Montana have played significant roles in bringing creative solutions to communities beleaguered by adolescent drug use and abuse problems. Because of their professional training and constant contact with troubled families and kids, they frequently witness problems before anyone else does.

Like everyone else, however, social service professionals must be made aware of the problems of alcohol and drug abuse and dependency. Because many professional degree programs do not address this issue, many communities have made special training for helping professionals a priority. "We really focused on the social service professionals when we recruited participants for our first training workshops here," said a counselor-therapist who helped design Bozeman's school-based prevention program. "We knew that their services to their own clients would be dramatically improved, and this has happened. We did not realize the extent to which our ability to cooperate with one another would improve, but it seems that 'professional turf' is not an issue anymore. We share a common concern and a common understanding now. Because helping professionals are ready to help, people get help faster and easier."

ANALYSIS OF THE MONTANA STORY

Credit for the successes in Montana must be given to thousands of individuals who have been planning, organizing, giving presentations, and offering direct services to young people and their families. Analysis of the dynamics of the Montana story, however, reveals three critical components in this mobilization effort: (1) the pressure applied by parents who felt the need for change, (2) the initial risks taken by Wendy's of Montana in sponsoring the state's first training events, and (3) as was true in Ohio, the model for action provided by an extensive series of professionally conducted training workshops.

Parents, a powerful pressure group

When teachers, probation officers, and other social service workers see a problem that demands attention, their efforts to make changes are frequently hampered by the very systems in which they work. Protocol demands that they duly consult each level of the hierarchy to request funds and staff time for new projects. The bureaucratic inertia that results can often dissipate creative energy long before plans reach the drawing board, much less the implementation stage.

Parents groups, however, are not hampered by such inertia. They are free to pick and choose among the community's resources and go directly to the top if necessary. When members of the parents group in Billings realized that social service professionals could not respond as quickly as the situation warranted, they tapped another community resource, a private businessperson.

Risk taking by the private sector

Decisiveness and a willingness to take risks are the hallmarks of successful businesspeople. When the board chairman of Wendy's of Montana decided that training geared toward solving adolescent alcohol and drug problems was an excellent idea, he was in a position to use the company's discretionary funds to pay not only the trainees' tuition but also their travel expenses to Minneapolis.

The fact that such training was a relatively unknown commodity in Montana at the time made it unlikely that a public institution would have taken such a risk without first doing extensive (and expensive) research to determine its relative merits. This kind of evaluation can take months or even years, depending on bureaucratic imperatives and city and state politics. Although Wendy's continues to provide excellent administrative support and consultation to other communities that want to sponsor their own training events, its initial risk taking in Billings was a key factor in the meteoric rise of drug programs and services throughout the state.

Training, a mandatory first step

By the spring of 1984, more than 1,500 people in Montana had been trained in community mobilization and early-intervention programming.

Again and again in Montana as elsewhere, this simple lesson

has been confirmed: The training of concerned adults in the community is a mandatory first step in changing the patterns of alcohol and drug use and abuse exhibited by young people in the community.

* * * * * * * *

Statewide efforts move on so many fronts and with such rapidity that individual efforts get lost in the recitation of accomplishments. In Chapter Eight, I'll focus on individuals. Although their stories are less global, they offer personal views and practical answers to questions commonly asked by people about to embark on their own campaigns against adolescent drug use and abuse.

CHAPTER EIGHT
Spotlight on Individual Efforts

Communities mobilize against adolescent drug use when one person after another starts working to solve the problem within his or her own sphere of influence, whether that sphere is a family, a neighborhood, a school district, or a state. In this chapter, I'll introduce 12 individuals who have done just that. Having worked with them, I feel their stories aptly illustrate the dynamics of mobilization and the four key components of drug programming: awareness and education presentations, identification and referral services, a continuum of counseling and treatment services, and support groups and activities. Equally important, their stories tell of individuals who have made the commitment, sought the education and tools, and found the allies needed to begin solving the problem of adolescent alcohol and drug use where it counts most, in their own communities.

PARENTS GROUPS

- Ann Forster, a parent from Wayzata, Minnesota, tells of her response to a potential personal and communitywide problem.

Rescuing kids from the fast lane

Ann Forster is not someone you'd call a naive parent isolated with her own unexplored fears about adolescent drug use. She had ten years' experience working in the field of adolescent chemical dependency, was living in a district with school-based drug programming, and over the years had formed personal connections with many helping professionals and community service providers. Nonetheless, when a junior high school counselor called her one spring day and said he thought that many of her child's classmates were experimenting with alcohol and other drugs, she found herself looking back over the past year with the same alarm and guilt that many less prepared parents feel. Looking forward offered no reassurance, either. Summer was fast approaching, and along with it would come the endless hours of "hanging out" and the spontaneous, impossible-to-supervise partying at the beach and in the woods.

Since she could find no ready-made alternatives to these activities, Forster used her training and determination to create one. She and a few other parents formed an impromptu parents group. They laid down some ground rules for their children and made it clear they would enforce them. Within a month, 30 other parents had asked to join the group. Together they altered the once-predictable course of the summer.

School-based programming alone cannot solve the problem. Parents can do much to modify their own and their children's attitudes about drug use by getting together, sharing information, seeking training, and defining their roles in the broader community effort. By sharing their knowledge and strengths with one another, parents can help their children in a variety of ways. Forster's parents group has become an effective, ongoing early-intervention and prevention force by setting rules and creating straight activities for kids and by establishing a continuing education program for both parents and kids.

"The first challenge I faced was a personal one," said Forster. "It's scary to call people whom you know only well enough to chat with at the grocery store and tell them that you're afraid their kids and yours may be in trouble with drugs. In this area, where families seldom stay longer than a few years and many parents, both mothers and fathers, work outside the home and the neighborhood, parents seldom have a chance to get to know one another.

"At first, only a few of us met to share our anxieties and

decide on a plan of action. We just wanted to minimize the risk for our own junior high kids by setting down some firm rules: no cigarettes, alcohol, or other drugs; 10 P.M. curfew; no loitering downtown during the day or at the beach, a known drug hangout, after dinner, etcetera. We never predicted that if we stuck to our guns with our own kids, other kids would feel left out. Whenever one of them said, 'Boy, my parents would love to slap those rules on me, too,' we said, 'OK, have them call us.' Within a month we'd heard from 30 parents who wanted to know what was up and how they could become involved.

"As the group expanded, meetings really drew upon my professional experience. I sensed so much pain and confusion just beneath the surface—this was especially true of the many single working mothers who were at their wits' end trying to work full-time and raise their children alone. Tremendous emotional supportiveness developed to alleviate the pain and confusion felt by these parents. It's not enough for parents to band together to try to control their children's behavior. We must band together to change our own attitudes and explore creative ways of dealing with our kids.

"We didn't concentrate solely on rule setting and discipline. That summer we also staged many straight activities, including barbecue parties and rafting expeditions, that involved parents with kids in new and positive ways. Kids started to open up about their anxieties and concerns. They didn't have to bury their insecurities under bravado and drugs any longer.

"Eventually, the focus of the parents group changed. Meetings are now open to the public. We still support one another personally, but we also offer general awareness and education presentations that are of interest to the entire family.

"We do not have a formal relationship with the school programs, but the communication between school staff members and parents has definitely improved. One junior high school principal said he could see the impact that the parents group was having on the kids in terms of their maturity and self-esteem. I guess I'd say that I'm guardedly optimistic about the long-range effects of our actions. We seem to have reached the kids who were starting to move in the fast lane, and I'm very glad we started now instead of waiting three or four years to wake up."

COMMUNITY VOLUNTEERS

■ Pam Allen and Mary Brock are community volunteers from St. Joseph, Missouri. Here they share their experiences in organizing their community much as they shared the task itself.

Gathering momentum for a community campaign

Volunteer organizations can be very effective in building the momentum needed to launch community mobilization campaigns. In numerous communities throughout the country, such organizations have proved formidable in their ability to rouse community concern and to encourage, cajole, and otherwise elicit the participation of many systems within the community.

This, in a nutshell, is what the volunteers and volunteer organizations in St. Joseph have done and are doing. Of course, many programs have come and gone in St. Joseph, just as they have in most communities beleaguered by adolescent alcohol and drug problems. The difference this time, residents say, is that they've discovered the value of networking and large-scale training. They are now experiencing the first wave of success from their initial awareness and education efforts. In the words of Pam Allen, a lifelong resident and active civic volunteer: "It's like watching the whole town come alive! After all these years something finally is working!" At this point, Allen is not willing to predict which programs will be the focus of the concerned systems' efforts. "We'll have to report back to you on the story of St. Joseph, but this is one community that hasn't wasted its time saying 'Ain't it a shame?'"

"So far, most of what is happening here is due to volunteer efforts," said Allen. "The members of the Juvenile Justice Coalition worked as volunteers; the Junior League has played and is still playing a vital role. Now that we've had an intensive weeklong training workshop, a great many people are volunteering their time and energy to community awareness and education programs. We do have three main objectives: to increase community awareness, to obtain more training, and to do a study to determine what we need here in the way of a continuum of counseling and treatment services. But I can't begin to describe in detail everything that's going on.

"It all began when the members of the Juvenile Justice Coalition, a volunteer group concerned with child advocacy issues, became aware that alcohol and drug use was a common denominator in the majority of cases they reviewed. They saw it as a root cause of crime, abuse, neglect, and accidents. Coalition chairman Mary Brock brought their concerns to the Junior League, of which she is also a member."

"Since child advocacy is one of the Junior League's primary concerns, its members supported us from the start," said Brock. "We could have encountered resistance from League members if we had just thrown the drug issue down on the table like a gauntlet. Instead, the Coalition offered them statistics and specific information about the kids in our town. It's important not to push or threaten people—they tend to get the wrong idea, like maybe you want to bring back Prohibition for all parents. That role model issue can be touchy."

"The Junior League decided to raise the funds needed to host a training workshop in St. Joseph. We provided funds so that many of our own members as well as many other people from the community could attend," said Allen. "The League joined forces with the Coalition's steering committee to cosponsor a one-day seminar conducted by Jim Crowley in order to sell the idea of a local workshop to social service professionals, school officials, the business community, and parents. From these groups the steering committee was able to raise funds and recruit participants for the workshop. Law enforcement personnel, volunteers, school teachers and administrators, parents, recovering people, and staff members from the Family Guidance Center attended the workshop. All of them were ready to do something without knowing what to do. It's been exciting to watch people cross all the social boundaries of the town to work together.

"I would say that almost every one of the 85 people who came to the first workshop is now working on some aspect of programming. Now we're planning another workshop because we realize that we need the help of some other people to keep things going and they'll need to be trained.

"Although the Junior League still has an important role to play, this effort is much broader than a League project. It has to be. We've had alcohol and drug programs come and go in St. Joseph for years; the problem, I think, has always been that too few people were aware of or became involved in them. This time, in the eight months since that first workshop, almost all staff members of the district schools have been through in-service training. Also, insight, abstinence support, and aftercare groups for students have been set up in the schools. Community volunteers are coming forward to cofacilitate these groups. Several local churches have sponsored drug and alcohol education classes for their own parishioners and the public. Local charities are looking at what their roles might be. We've conducted in-service training for state and private hospital staffs. Parents are also getting involved through the Caring Family groups.

"The Junior League as a volunteer organization raised the funds to send people to training, and now these 85 trained people are carrying the work forward. Watching the network grow at this stage is wonderful! Special things are happening between people in this town. Everyone is starting to take responsibility for solving a problem that is very big and very old."

SCHOOL COUNSELORS

■ Joe Baer, a high school counselor from South Milwaukee, Wisconsin, offers advice on developing a school-based program.

Doing it right from the beginning

Drug and alcohol programming is off to a good start in South Milwaukee schools thanks to the low-key but persistent efforts of high school counselor Joe Baer and a volunteer faculty committee. Concerned about what he saw as one of the most pressing but ignored problems confronting students and their school counselors, two years ago Baer began steering the committee toward taking a look at the issue of student drug abuse. They decided to do a survey of student drug use patterns and parental awareness levels and attitudes. Although the survey was carried out with very little fanfare, the results dropped the jaws and opened the eyes of many administrators. Baer sought training at Community Intervention, Inc., in Minneapolis and then, with the administration's backing, approached the school board to ask for its approval of new policies and programs. Soon after, new policies were instated and new programs established. Baer now spends about half his time coordinating a K-12 drug and alcohol intervention program in his district. His number one strategy: Train the counselors.

"To really get somewhere with this problem takes time. There's no shortcut, so you might as well do it right from the beginning. I think most concerned school personnel have a pretty good idea of what kind of resistance they will encounter and what it might take to break through it. Since most of them know very little about adolescent drug problems and programs, I would say that their first step should be to obtain training.

"If they also take the time to do a survey among parents and students, they'll have the analytical data and the facts they need to gain their administration's approval. It makes no sense for them to get into this issue if they don't have the undivided support of their administrators. In South Milwaukee, the survey accomplished a lot. We didn't have to go through any elaborate procedures to get approval to do the survey. It was a pretty low-key operation—until we revealed the results. That's when the mouths dropped open and the eyes opened, too.

"When the survey showed that about 50% of the sixth graders in the district had used alcohol but that few, if any, of the parents were aware of the fact, it stimulated a lot of interest and concern among parents. Technically, we were proceeding with some aspects of programming even before we won the school board's approval because so many parents and students were coming to us. It wasn't long before we received the approval we hoped for.

"The way I see it, no high school can expect to have good programs unless counselors have been trained. In South

Milwaukee, student support groups are usually cofacilitated by one counselor and one teacher rather than two teachers. This way the school doesn't have to hire substitute teachers for the sake of the program. One counselor from each of the senior high, junior high, and elementary grades also receives advanced training in the field of adolescent chemical dependency. Then they share what they have learned with others. Basic training is offered to school nurses, other staff members, clergy, and other people from the community who want to help.

"Counselors definitely need special training because, even now, not enough professional degree programs are giving their graduates the kind of background they need to be able to cope with the adolescent drug problem. Counselors can be very effective if they add this special training to the education they received in graduate school."

■ Carolynn Brown is a high school counselor and Ann Cattau is an elementary school teacher in the Neenah, Wisconsin, school district. Both believe that a successful school-based program "starts where you are" and grows from there.

Creating effective agents of change

When Carolynn Brown and Ann Cattau first became involved in the issue of student chemical abuse a few years ago, both were working in schools in Neenah—Brown with high school students and Cattau with elementary school students. They were concerned because a problem that pervaded their daily work lives had received so little attention from the community. They were frustrated by their inability to deal with the problem in the school setting.

Today, Brown is still working with high school students and Cattau with elementary school students, but they are also the chairperson and vice-chairperson, respectively, of the Neenah Community Action Committee. As school staff members, they have worked to set up programs within the schools. As community members who have been trained to deal with this issue, they are working for change in the community. Both had the credibility, sought the training, and possessed the hope and commitment they needed to become effective agents of change.

"Out of a sense of frustration about being unable somehow to deal effectively with young drug users, a diverse group of people met in March 1982 to form the Neenah Community Action Committee," said Brown. "I joined the committee at this first meeting. As a school counselor, I saw this problem every day. However, none of us who joined the committee knew much about chemical dependency or had any idea of what approach to the problem might be effective. We were just casting around, looking for something.

"In June, three of us, including Ann, attended an intensive training workshop at Community Intervention, Inc., in Minneapolis. When we returned, Ann and I knew we wanted to set up an early-intervention program in the schools as soon as possible. We made presentations about what we'd learned to the school administrators and won their support. We had finally succeeded in changing our own views; we no longer believe that drug use is a hopeless problem with no solution. I think we had credibility with the school administration because we worked in the school system; that made a lot of difference.

"But since we were also part of the committee, we were able to get the schools and the community working together from the start. This is really an important factor. The push came from the community, not just the schools. This problem is and should be a community concern. Schools, I think, should respond to community needs. Schools are reactive, not proactive. The community did and still does support the programs by providing volunteers and by financing training scholarships for both school and community people.

"Because I was involved as both a school counselor and a community member, I was able to plant seeds in both places. I could also be more aggressive after I stepped forward and volunteered to act as project coordinator for the committee. Ann is also a concerned person wearing several hats. She is a teacher, vice-chairperson of the committee, and president of the Neenah Education Association. That made a difference in terms of the cooperation we received from school personnel. The association was one of the first groups to provide funding for the training of teachers.

"All hasn't gone smoothly, of course. I don't think any

reasonable person could expect that. Before we went to training, we had no idea of what to do. As counselors and teachers, we all had avoided dealing with the problem. Since training, there is no question that we have become much more effective in our work. People feel better about themselves when they can make a positive difference in their own and others' lives."

PROGRAM COORDINATORS

- Mary Lou Jensen is the coordinator of the Chemical Awareness and Employee Assistance Program for the Minnetonka, Minnesota, school district. She works hard to keep the schools and community engaged in a cooperative venture to solve their adolescent drug problem.

Building programs one step at a time

Minnetonka, a small town/suburb located a few miles west of Minneapolis, seems at first glance to be a kind of "programming utopia." Back in 1976, school personnel and community people launched their programs simultaneously out of shared concern for their youth. School staff and administrators and community volunteers continue to support a wide range of school-based programs. These programs are augmented by equally vital community efforts. Through the years, various community task forces have focused on special concerns, including education for parents, networks of parents groups, community awareness, special needs of elementary school students, business-industry-church-school liaisons, and chemical-free activities for young people and their families.

Community support has become so pervasive that when the school district faced severe funding cutbacks two years ago, the school-based drug programs emerged relatively unscathed. Thanks to the efforts of many volunteers, these programs are still going strong on a budget that provides for only one salaried employee.

Compared with communities still engaged in dramatic struggles against denial, inertia, blaming, or political game playing, Minnetonka does make the process look easy. Looks, however, can be deceiving. According to Mary Lou Jensen, the coordinator of the Chemical Awareness and Employee Assistance Program for Minnetonka schools and the district's sole salaried program employee, maintaining strong community/school rapport involves hard work. It demands ceaseless communication, a willingness to "advertise" both the problems and the efforts to solve them, encouragement of volunteers by providing them with training, an openness to new ideas, and a nitty-gritty faith in the process.

"In 1976, I certainly never imagined that our programs would grow like they have," said Jensen. "When I look back, I see that we always took just one small step at a time. We moved on to new areas as the need became apparent. People would pop up with suggestions and insights, others would come forward to help, and pretty soon the suggestions were implemented. It's been a rather amazing process!

"In the beginning, just two other teachers and I were looking for a solution to this problem. Three people! We saw that a neighboring community [Wayzata] had good programs, so we followed its ideas back to their source and eventually had Jim Crowley come to talk to us. Following this meeting, we decided to form a committee and began to recruit school personnel, community representatives, and parents. There has always been good rapport among these groups.

"But maintaining rapport means keeping people involved in the programs. We've recruited parents and volunteers by offering to send them to training. We can raise the funds to pay their tuition from private citizens, businesses, and churches because we've prepared the ground by advertising what we are trying to do.

"You must be willing to promote what you are doing to solve the problem. If you are visible, people will come forward to help you. Because of their ideas, our programs have grown and evolved. For example, at the end of one school year the kids in my aftercare support groups wanted to know what they were going to do over the summer. I agreed to meet with them every so often to talk about the issues we had been discussing in group. Then several parents offered to help with the logistics. Pretty soon we were having parties and were urging more parents to get involved. That's how the Summertime

Turn-On Program originated. When funds for that program were cut, we were able to obtain replacement funds from private foundations because people there knew about the program and supported the idea behind it.

"Part of this 'advertising' is really community awareness programming, which in Minnetonka is one of the ongoing tasks of our original committee. This year five subcommittees are focusing on establishing a crisis center, a safe house, and a hotline and on improving elementary-level programs.

"We have established our credibility in the community and we have a whole range of programs in operation, yet I am the only salaried person in the district's school-based program. How do we do it? Community involvement. It doesn't matter how few in number you are in the beginning. You build support out of your own commitment, even if you are running one small program in one school building. Word spreads. If you help the members of one family, they will share the information with others who need help. Those people will call you. Pretty soon you have a core of interested people and proof that you are serving a valuable function. Then you can take another step."

■ Connie Tooley was the coordinator of the Student and Employee Assistance Program for the Rochester, Minnesota, school district. She is now the employee assistance counselor at Rochester Methodist Hospital. While program coordinator, she discovered that schools play a significant role in the development of community services for young drug users.

Keeping the lines of communication open

The need for adolescent drug programming in Rochester schools had been apparent and accepted as early as 1977 when Connie Tooley, a registered nurse and certified chemical dependency practitioner, began working with the Chemical Dependency Services of the Zumbro Valley Mental Health Center to develop the Student and Employee Assistance Program for the school district. Many other needs were not apparent then, at least not to the community at large. By demonstrating the need for new services, the schools raised the level of awareness in the community, which responded by creating the necessary services. According to Tooley, further expansion of the continuum of care for young users now depends on whether the schools, the community, and the new services maintain close communication.

"Before we even started the school program, we knew we would be flooding the community agencies," said Tooley. "Services for adolescents were fairly limited in Rochester at that time, but you have to show the need before you get the program. Almost no one builds a ten-room house unless he or she needs the space.

"As the student assistance aspect of the program gained support within the school system, it became obvious that assessment was the number one priority. In my opinion, the problems of adolescents are much more difficult to diagnose than those of adults. Chemical dependency services that ignore adolescent growth and development issues aren't effective. Neither are social and psychological services that don't look at chemical use. We worked with several area agencies to design an assessment program, which is now operated by a youth agency. It combines both lecture and group discussion with parental participation and peer interaction, and it works very well.

"But all the way along, many counselors encountered clients who didn't fit the mold when it came to available forms of treatment. What about kids in the early stages of dependency? What about kids who weren't sick enough to be sent out of town for intensive inpatient treatment but clearly were harmfully involved with chemicals? Out of their need emerged the Zumbro Valley Mental Health Center's Teens Program. Counselors and assessment personnel now refer a student to this program when his or her profile shows an unclear but worrisome pattern of chemical abuse.

"The need for a third type of service became apparent when we saw that a significant number of kids, especially junior high students, weren't dependent yet but were starting to abuse drugs for want of 'social competence.' The same youth agency that provides assessment services took on the job of working with these kids in a program that focused on acquiring social skills, making decisions, and developing a positive self-concept.

"At the same time, as more and more chemically dependent youth were identified, parents began asking why they had to send their children out of town for treatment when the city obviously had the resources to establish an excellent facility of its own. Establishing a treatment unit for chemically dependent adolescents at the Mayo Clinic was really a total community effort involving parents, concerned clinic staff members, and local agency personnel.

"For every programmatic step we wanted to take, you see, we had to demonstrate a clear and verifiable need. It would never have worked for those of us in the chemical dependency field to have said, 'Hey! What this city needs is an inpatient program, a school program, and a whole range of services.' You can't launch a program without broad-based support. Without the support of the school, we could never have gotten started. Without the support of the community, we would never have created the services we need.

"Three things have been important in this process. One is training. If you want the program to be accepted, you must start training people—school personnel, of course, but also the staff members of community agencies and parents. The more training, education, and outreach you do in the early stages of the program, the easier it will be later for you to get the local services you need.

"The second important element has been the program's excellent advisory board. It's made up of professionals from the Mayo Clinic and the Olmsted County Medical Group, a clergyperson, teachers, administrators, parents, students, and representatives from local agencies. The board plays an essential role in keeping the lines of communication open so that agency people in the community learn what our needs are and vice versa. This exchange of information is a very important aid in raising the community's level of awareness.

"The third factor, then, overlaps the other two. It is communication among all the people who are concerned and involved. Nothing will sabotage a program sooner than the inability to relay information back and forth. For example, assessment counselors have to know about the kids' problems in school, and we have to know how to integrate their suggestions into our school support systems. Lack of communication could cause a significant problem, so we spend a lot of time cultivating trust and cooperation between us and these agencies. The advisory board helps here, as does training. Close communication changes attitudes, raises the level of awareness, and points out people's responsibility to do something, regardless of the system from which they come or in which they work."

- Ken Kelly is the director of the CA/RE (Chemical Abuse/Responsive Education) program in the Great Falls, Montana, school district. He has found that the strong working relationship between the schools and the courts provides both systems with the necessary tools to help the community's adolescents.

Closing loopholes in policies and procedures

In December 1983, the representatives of all city and county law enforcement agencies, the juvenile justice system, and the county attorney's office of Great Falls signed an agreement outlining the way in which these systems would handle minors found to be intoxicated or in possession of or driving while under the influence of alcohol. Basically, this simple document streamlines the procedures by which a young person is routed through these systems to receive the help he or she needs. In accordance with this agreement, all law enforcement officers must refer young offenders to the juvenile intake department, and one court and one judge (instead of three courts and judges) hear the cases of all young offenders. The consequences of alcohol use by minors are no longer left to a judge's discretion. They have been spelled out and include assignment to school-based insight groups, assessment, and possible mandatory treatment for chemical dependency.

This agreement has effectively closed many of the loopholes that had inadvertently enabled kids to continue abusing alcohol even after they had come to the attention of the police. It brought about a much-needed clarification of bureaucratic procedures in Great Falls. It also marked the culmination of a complex and difficult three-year campaign to win the cooperation of these key systems, according to CA/RE program director Ken Kelly. This campaign serves as a perfect illustration of how to mobilize key systems by building a ground swell of community support and using perseverance, patience, and a nonthreatening style of politicking.

"It is very exciting to see what happens when people start realizing that they can influence their public officials to sit down and really work on a problem," said Kelly. "A little success fires people's interest, and as interest grows, people work harder. We have done a fairly good job here in Great Falls of publicizing our successes and letting people know that the programs are working.

"Some of our success is due to the careful selection of workshop participants. We invited and provided scholarship funds for key community people and staff members of social service agencies, but we also looked for people who were sensitive to the issue of adolescent chemical use and who could work from the same philosophical base. That was very important here, especially in the early stages.

"We had to be able to agree on fundamentals because getting the key law enforcement and juvenile system agencies to sign this agreement involved a sustained three-year effort. We had to convince them that a great many people in the community were taking adolescent chemical abuse seriously, that the old attitude 'Kids will be kids, and kids are going to drink no matter what we do' wasn't acceptable anymore. Obviously, just two or three or even a dozen people wouldn't have had much impact. As it was, however, if someone from an agency balked and refused to attend our presentations, hundreds of key community people signed a petition formally requesting that person's and that agency's participation.

"During a five-month period, we often met with these reluctant people individually and in groups. Trained members of the community core team and CA/RE program members presented the facts of adolescent chemical use, abuse, and dependency here in Great Falls. We discussed the fact that very few minors were ever arrested on minor DUI charges and the fact that bar and liquor store owners were rarely, if ever, prosecuted for selling alcohol to minors. We confronted them with testimonies from recovering kids who pinpointed which bars and stores sold to minors without checking identification.

"We gathered support as we went. The community core team, for example, asked the Tavern Owners Association to urge its members to uphold the no-alcohol-sales-to-minors laws, which it did formally. We even persuaded the Montana Revenue Service to offer the public free presentations on these laws. All these small pieces of support together made a pretty powerful whole. I think some agencies thought that if they appeased us, we would eventually go away. We didn't. We continued pressing for their undivided support.

"It all could have blown up, though, at many different points. Blaming and divisiveness were rampant among agency personnel, some of whom wanted to work with us and some of whom did not. Some of the law enforcement people felt justified in turning kids loose right away because they didn't think the courts were doing as much as they should. Three different courts were handling juvenile cases at that time, and they all dealt with the problem in different ways. In trying to come up with a policy and procedure agreement, we scrapped many drafts and began again several times. By maintaining a positive, nonthreatening approach and not giving up, we eventually succeeded, but only after lengthy negotiations.

"The end result is simply that *all* minors picked up for breaking the alcohol laws are sent to the intake department of the juvenile justice system. If they are first-time offenders, they have a choice: They can either attend a school-based insight group or go before a justice of the peace, who most likely will refer them to an insight group anyway. Second-time offenders are sent directly to the justice of the peace, who uses a slightly heavier hand this time to encourage them to undergo assessment for a serious chemical problem. For a third offense, the minor is sent to the county attorney's office for possible prosecution as a youth in need of supervision, at which point treatment may be made mandatory.

"In Montana, alcohol cases are handled differently than cases involving other illegal substances. Kids caught breaking the laws regarding other drugs are sent directly to the county attorney's office for prosecution. Now, however, this office has agreed to refer these young people to the school-based insight groups instead of prosecuting them.

"The entire court-school relationship has done more than a school-based program could have on its own. The CA/RE program could not have handled the 200 kids referred to insight groups during the 1982-1983 school year, or the 60 some who attended last summer, without the help of many people in the community. For example, trained volunteers from the community and professionals from treatment centers and other agencies facilitate the summer groups. Neither the city nor the county has to pay for their help. *That* kind of community support makes things happen."

SOCIAL SERVICE PROFESSIONALS

■ Janet Hawkes and Doug Wentz do the same kind of work in two of the 12 Regional Councils on Alcoholism (RCAs) in Ohio. Over time, each has discovered that communities and schools can change dramatically when chemical problems are openly addressed and that the intervention-to-prevention approach works best in dealing with these problems.

Developing skills, then letting go

Both the Region Ten Council on Alcoholism (RTCA) and the Northeastern Ohio Regional Council on Alcoholism (NEORCA) were established in 1974 under the auspices of the Ohio Department of Health. The councils are mandated to work on the prevention of alcohol problems, but people weren't exactly beating down the office doors demanding services. The need existed; of that, the RCA and the State of Ohio had no doubt. The dilemma was how to motivate people and teach them the skills they need to work for change.

After many years of trying different methods and having varying degrees of success, today both Janet Hawkes, regional education director for the five-county Region Ten, and Doug Wentz, regional prevention coordinator of NEORCA's four-county Region Eleven, agree that the most effective method has been to identify potential community resource people and develop their skills through intensive training. When people in communities are brought together to work on programs they all support, many of the existing rifts and conceptual barriers that separate them can be mended. The helping professionals at NEORCA and RTCA have found that while they don't have to be passive, they can't presume to tell communities how to run their programs. Hawkes and Wentz have learned that a major part of the job is knowing when to let go.

"Over the past five years much of my effort at NEORCA has gone into building a networking system," said Wentz. "I match people who have problems with people who have solutions. I connect school superintendents with superintendents, nurses with nurses, schools with schools, and I let people help one another. That is what has worked best.

"People do have to solve their problems in their own ways. Every program must be tailored to meet each community's needs. I can offer some ideas, but I can't solve a community's problems on my own. I learned this the hard way by walking into schools and agencies and saying, in effect, 'Hey! This is the answer to your problems. *This* is what you have to do.' People were usually very nice. They seemed to accept my ideas at the time, but as often as not they stashed them in a drawer somewhere soon after I left.

"All of us here had to learn to talk to people first, find out the focus of their concerns, and then 'develop' these people into resources for their communities. Developing resources means giving tools to people and that means education. Then people can tailor programs to suit themselves.

"Yet we were still focusing on too narrow a field without knowing it. We were focused just on alcoholism and just on prevention. We didn't have the knowledge or confidence we needed to branch out into intervention, which we saw as something quite separate. Any talk about other drugs would have meant we were invading another agency's turf. All the helping agencies had their own turf. The big watershed occurred in 1981, when we sponsored our first weeklong training workshop and invited all kinds of people from these diverse agencies. We found out that we really were working on different aspects of the same problem and that we could work together. Now we can be resources for one another. We're all plugged into the same network. Chemical abuse is chemical abuse, whether you're talking about alcohol or other drugs.

Intervention is at the heart of prevention at many levels."

"I came to Region Ten with a different perspective," said Hawkes. "I had always believed in early intervention; I don't believe people—young or old—have to 'reach bottom' before they can get help. I just couldn't envision how I could get enough people in the right places to work effectively on early intervention. The Greater Cleveland School Superintendents Association's 1981 announcement of support for community and school drug programs inspired us. Six school districts in my region had formed a compact arrangement to provide vocational education to their students. They used this compact to work for administrative support for school-based programs. On a smaller scale, they duplicated the efforts of the Superintendents Association. The success of this effort gave us at Region Ten the initial wedge we needed to help other area communities plan their intervention-to-prevention program strategies.

"One of our main ways of supporting community efforts is to cooperate with local school districts in cosponsoring Community Intervention, Inc., workshops throughout the five counties we serve. This pays off in immediate results in school-based programming—starting them, bolstering them, improving them—and creates a ripple effect throughout other systems within the community. Trainees become articulate advocates of change, and many are motivated enough to give their free time to outreach efforts in other systems and other communities. For example, school principals link up to help other districts, and helping professionals give seminars for other agencies. If school-based intervention-to-prevention programs weren't reaping positive results, we wouldn't enjoy the success we've had in raising the private grant funds used to train people to work in school-based programs. But they *have* been successful, and the communities and private foundations are supporting them on a continuing basis.

"My position at Region Ten is gratifying. I help such a wide range of people acquire the tools they need to help themselves. The flip side of this is that after I link people with training and with one another, they take over their own programming efforts and I don't have to hand-hold them anymore. When I'm successful and when the Regional Council's programs are successful, people don't need to rely on me after a while. They become the experts in their own schools and communities."

PROBATION OFFICERS

- Jerry Retar, a probation officer from Lake County, Ohio, tells how a school-based program was adapted to a court setting to meet the needs of area young people.

Offering a promising alternative

Until 1980, the juvenile justice system in Lake County was no more prepared than any other community agency to deal with adolescent drug abuse as a separate entity. It operated under the assumption that excessive use of drugs by young offenders is merely a symptom of more important social, family, and economic problems. Questions about chemical use habits went unasked. When time and again court-imposed probation and detention proved ineffective, the inability to help the very people they were trained, hired, and working hard to help left probation officers feeling helpless, frustrated, and cynical.

Then a newly appointed judge, Richard A. Hoose, encouraged Jerry Retar and another probation officer to set up an education program for young DWI offenders. The two officers contacted the Region Twelve division of the Regional Council on Alcoholism and were invited to attend an intensive weeklong training workshop. They began to ask questions. They set up a range of successful programs that allowed them to use the "big sticks" of court-imposed probation and detention in more sophisticated ways.

The juvenile justice system was among the first social service organizations in Lake County to deal directly with adolescent drug abuse. It was at one time, in Retar's words, "practically the only show in town." The probation department's programs changed the role of the juvenile justice system in the community and the public's perception of the probation department. They also helped make the community aware of the need for a broader base of services.

"I don't think that anyone can work in social services without really wanting to help people," said Retar. "When you can't or don't know how to deal with some of their problems, this caring is buried under layers of cynicism and pessimism. That's why it's exciting to discover a method that works.

"The people in our department are basically conservative and skeptical. We know better than to latch onto every new programming fad that comes along, but those of us who went to training had confidence in the intervention approach right away. It was practical; we could start by using what we'd learned in the training workshop and by asking the kids in our caseloads a lot of direct questions. Soon we were doing what amounted to preliminary assessments, making referrals either to the drug and alcohol education class or to out-of-town treatment centers, since nothing was available here. The parent support groups and the aftercare programs all evolved slowly as we recognized the need for them and trained more and more staff members in the probation, intake, and detention departments of the juvenile justice system.

"Today we see many more kids whose problems are not yet severe. Now kids who may be truant or drinking at home against their parents' wishes but haven't yet been in trouble with the police are being referred to us by parents, schools, and other agencies. I think this change has come about for three reasons. First, Lake County is smaller than urban areas such as Cleveland, where the probation officers have all they can do to keep up with the serious offenders. Second, these programs have strengthened our relationships with the schools and other agencies. Third, our public image has changed; we aren't just the 'last resort for bad kids.' People know that we want, and have really been able, to help young people.

"Whether our clients are referred by the courts, the police, parents, or other agencies, we screen them for possible drug problems and then decide whether assessment or probation is appropriate. We offer help in the form of drug education or referral to assessment to kids who have drug problems. If they refuse to cooperate and work on their problems, we can then recommend a stay in the detention center. As a court agency, we have this advantage. This is our 'big stick.' Because the staff of the detention center is also trained to deal with drug problems, these kids don't slip out that door, either.

"Our role in the community has definitely changed, and

continues to change, because the community is changing. In the early days, we were one of the few agencies that could deal with the drug problems of kids, so we were goaded by the feeling of having to save everybody and do it by next week! Now we have the help of a variety of services in Lake County, including a treatment center and a counseling and assessment agency, plus the cooperation of the schools and parents. In a personal sense, our jobs have become easier. We no longer feel that we must save everybody and we have learned that it certainly can't be done overnight."

* * * * * * * *

APPENDIX A
Selected Sources of Information

Publications from government agencies

An abundance of literature and statistical surveys that focus on drug and alcohol problems can be obtained from the following government agencies:

- National Institute on Drug Abuse (NIDA)
  Write to:
  National Clearinghouse for Drug Abuse Information
  P.O. Box 416
  Kensington, Maryland 20795

- National Institute on Alcoholism and Alcohol Abuse (NIAAA)
  Write to:
  National Clearinghouse for Alcohol Information
  P.O. Box 2345
  Rockville, Maryland 20852

Books

The following books provide useful information about the children of alcoholics and the ways in which concerned persons can help these children:

- *It Will Never Happen to Me!*
  By Claudia Black, MSW. 183 pages. 1982, M.A.C., Printing and Publications Division, 1850 High Street, Denver, CO 80218. $7.95, paperback.

- *Broken Bottles, Broken Dreams: Understanding and Helping the Children of Alcoholics*
  By Charles Deutsch. 213 pages. 1982, Teachers College Press, Columbia University, 1234 Amsterdam Avenue, New York, NY 10027. $13.95, paperback; $17.95, hardcover.

Publications from Alcoholics Anonymous

Alcoholics Anonymous is a self-help organization that publishes current information on all aspects of alcoholism—personal, family, social. For a list of current publications and prices, write to:

- Alcoholics Anonymous World Services, Inc.
  Box 459, Grand Central Station
  New York, NY 10163

APPENDIX B

Sample Surveys of Drug Use Patterns

The following sample surveys of student drug use patterns were derived from a wide variety of sources and appear in two different formats. You may select questions from either or both samples for your own survey.

Survey A focuses on the types and amounts of drugs used and is compatible with the national surveys conducted by the National Institute on Drug Abuse. This compatibility aids in the correlation of local survey data with national statistics. This may be especially useful if the governing body being approached is impressed with such statistical analyses.

Survey B focuses on drug-related attitudes and experiences. It elicits more personal responses than Survey A and thus may be more compatible with the preliminary assessment procedures used in your early-intervention program. The governing body may find this approach more relevant than the other if its concern is with individuals, especially the adolescents in your community.

Preceding the two surveys is a general information sheet for compiling the demographics on your survey audience. It can be used with either sample survey or with your own composite survey.

The questions provided here serve only as a resource pool for constructing a survey on the alcohol and drug use patterns, attitudes, and experiences of the young people in your community. Many factors, the initial one being whether or not the task force clearly understands the reason for doing this survey as a part of the needs assessment, will determine which questions you include, how you phrase them, and how you interpret and present the data.

General information

1. Circle your present age: 12 13 14 15 16 17 18 19

2. Check your sex: ____ male ____ female

3. Circle your present grade level: 6 7 8 9 10 11 12

4. What is your racial or ethnic background? (Check one answer only.)

   ____ White, Caucasian   ____ Oriental, Asian-American
   ____ Black, Afro-   ____ Hispanic
         American   ____ Other (please specify)
   ____ American Indian   _____

5. How many school sports do you play?

   ____ None   ____ Two
   ____ One   ____ Three or more

6. Do you participate in school activities such as the newspaper, student government, science or language club, debate, orchestra, choir, or drama?

   ____ Not at all   ____ Quite a bit
   ____ A little   ____ A great deal
   ____ Somewhat

7. How well are you doing in school?

   ____ Well above average   ____ Below average
   ____ Above average   ____ Well below average
   ____ Average

Other general questions included in drug surveys follow:

- What is your religious affiliation?
- How often do you attend church services?
- Do you participate in recreational activities and organizations outside of school?
- Are your parents separated or divorced?
- Do you have an after-school job?
- What level of education does your father and mother have?

Survey A

The following questions call for a frequency response. Instruct students to check one of the following choices for each question.

___ Never
___ 1-2 times
___ 3-5 times
___ 6-9 times
___ 10-19 times
___ 20-39 times
___ 40 or more times

Since the choices remain constant throughout this survey, they have not been repeated after each question. The use of a computer-scored answer sheet is recommended to simplify the recording and compiling of statistics.

The following statement, or something similar, can be used to introduce this survey to students:

> We want to learn about young people's actual experiences with and attitudes toward alcohol and other drugs. We hope that you will answer all the questions, but if you feel that you cannot answer a question honestly, leave it blank. You can be certain that no attempt will be made to connect your name with your answers and that all answers will be kept strictly confidential.

1. How many times in your lifetime have you had a drink? (A drink is a 4-ounce glass of wine, a bottle or can of beer, a shot glass of liquor, or a mixed drink.)
2. How many times during the past 12 months have you had a drink?
3. How many times during the past 30 days have you had a drink?
4. How many times in your lifetime have you used marijuana (grass, pot) or hashish (hash, hash oil)?
5. How many times during the past 12 months have you used marijuana or hashish?
6. How many times during the past 30 days have you used marijuana or hashish?
7. How many times in your lifetime have you used LSD

(acid) and/or hallucinogens such as mescaline, peyote, psilocybin, or PCP?
8. How many times during the past 12 months have you used LSD and/or hallucinogens?
9. How many times during the past 30 days have you used LSD and/or hallucinogens?
10. How many times in your lifetime have you used cocaine (coke)?
11. How many times during the past 12 months have you used cocaine?
12. How many times during the past 30 days have you used cocaine?
13. Amphetamines are sometimes prescribed by physicians to help people lose weight or increase their energy. Other names for amphetamines include uppers, ups, speed, bennies, dexies, pep pills, and diet pills. How many times in your lifetime have you taken amphetamines without a prescription?
14. How many times during the past 12 months have you taken amphetamines without a prescription?
15. How many times during the past 30 days have you taken amphetamines without a prescription?
16. Tranquilizers are sometimes prescribed by physicians to calm people down, quiet their nerves, or relax their muscles. Librium, Valium, and Miltown are tranquilizers. How many times in your lifetime have you taken tranquilizers without a prescription?
17. How many times during the past 12 months have you taken tranquilizers without a prescription?
18. How many times during the past 30 days have you taken tranquilizers without a prescription?
19. Barbiturates are sometimes prescribed by physicians to help people relax or sleep. Other names for barbiturates include downs, downers, goofballs, yellows, reds, blues, and rainbows. How many times in your lifetime have you taken barbiturates without a prescription?
20. How many times during the past 12 months have you taken barbiturates without a prescription?
21. How many times during the past 30 days have you taken barbiturates without a prescription?

22. Methaqualone (Quaalude) is a sedative sometimes prescribed by physicians to help people relax. Other names for Quaaludes include quads, ludes, and soapers. How many times in your lifetime have you taken Quaaludes without a prescription?
23. How many times during the past 12 months have you taken Quaaludes without a prescription?
24. How many times during the past 30 days have you taken Quaaludes without a prescription?
25. How many times in your lifetime have you sniffed glue, breathed the contents of aerosol spray cans, or inhaled any other gases or sprays to get high?
26. How many times during the past 12 months have you sniffed glue, breathed the contents of aerosol spray cans, or inhaled any other gases or sprays to get high?
27. How many times during the past 30 days have you sniffed glue, breathed the contents of aerosol spray cans, or inhaled any other gases or sprays to get high?
28. Heroin is a narcotic that is never prescribed by physicians. How many times in your lifetime have you used heroin (smack, horse, scag)?
29. How many times during the past 12 months have you used heroin?
30. How many times during the past 30 days have you used heroin?
31. The narcotics methadone, opium (Paregoric), morphine, codeine, Demerol, Talwin, and laudanum are sometimes prescribed by physicians to help people who are in intense pain. How many times in your lifetime have you taken any of these narcotics without a prescription?
32. How many times during the past 12 months have you taken any of these narcotics without a prescription?
33. How many times during the past 30 days have you taken any of these narcotics without a prescription?

Survey B

1. Which of the following problems has your use of alcohol, marijuana, or other drugs caused? (Check all answers that apply.)

    ___ Never use alcohol or other drugs
    ___ Damaged relationship with my parents
    ___ Damaged relationship with my girlfriend/boyfriend
    ___ Damaged relationships with my friends
    ___ Damaged relationships with teachers and/or coaches
    ___ Involvement with people I think are bad influences
    ___ Damaged school and/or job performance
    ___ Trouble with school authorities for breaking school rules related to drugs
    ___ Trouble with school authorities for breaking school rules not related to drugs
    ___ Less interest in sports and/or other school activities
    ___ Less emotional stability
    ___ Less energy
    ___ Interference with my ability to think clearly
    ___ Other harmful emotional and/or mental effects
    ___ Physical illness or injury
    ___ Unsafe driving
    ___ Trouble with the police
    ___ None of the problems listed

2. In what grade did you first drink alcohol without your parents' knowledge?

    ___ Never drink alcohol   ___ Grade 9
    ___ Grade 6 or below   ___ Grade 10
    ___ Grade 7   ___ Grade 11
    ___ Grade 8   ___ Grade 12

3. In what grade did you first use marijuana or any other illegal or nonprescribed drug?

    ___ Never use drugs   ___ Grade 9
    ___ Grade 6 or below   ___ Grade 10
    ___ Grade 7   ___ Grade 11
    ___ Grade 8   ___ Grade 12

The following set of answers can be used for questions 4 through 12.

___ Never
___ Rarely
___ Occasionally
___ Usually
___ Always

4. How often do you drink beer, wine, or hard liquor at parties where no adults are present?
5. How often do you drink beer, wine, or hard liquor at home on special occasions such as birthdays or on special holidays such as Thanksgiving and Christmas?
6. How often do you drink beer, wine, or hard liquor while in a car?
7. How often do you drink beer, wine, or hard liquor at places where kids hang around and no adults are present?
8. How often do you drink beer, wine, or hard liquor at parties where your own or someone else's parents are present?
9. How often do you drink beer, wine, or hard liquor during or after school activities such as football games and dances when adults are not present or cannot see you?
10. How often do you drink beer, wine, or hard liquor at school before classes begin?
11. How often do you drink beer, wine, or hard liquor at school after classes have ended?
12. How often do you drink beer, wine, or hard liquor at home when your parents don't know you are drinking?
13. How often do you think your parents know when you've been drinking? (Check one answer only.)

    ___ Never
    ___ A few times
    ___ Half the time
    ___ Most of the time
    ___ Always
    ___ Never drink alcohol

14. When you drink, where do you obtain the alcohol? (Check all answers that apply.)
    ___ From the alcohol my parents keep at home
    ___ From friends my own age
    ___ At a liquor store
    ___ At a grocery store
    ___ At a bar or tavern
    ___ From someone who is old enough to buy alcohol legally
    ___ Never drink alcohol

The following set of answers can be used for questions 15, 16, and 17.
    ___ Very difficult
    ___ Fairly difficult
    ___ Fairly easy
    ___ Very easy

15. How difficult do you think it would be for you to obtain marijuana if you wanted it?
16. How difficult do you think it would be for you to obtain amphetamines if you wanted them?
17. How difficult do you think it would be for you to obtain cocaine if you wanted it?

The following set of answers can be used for questions 18, 19, and 20.
    ___ Yes
    ___ No
    ___ Haven't used during the past 12 months

18. At any time during the past 12 months have you thought that you should reduce or stop your use of alcohol?
19. At any time during the past 12 months have you thought that you should reduce or stop your use of marijuana?
20. At any time during the past 12 months have you thought that you should reduce or stop your use of any other drug?

21. Here are some reasons people give for not using or for stopping their use of marijuana. Check all the reasons that are true for you.

___ Never use marijuana
___ Concern about possible psychological damage
___ Concern about possible physical illness or injury
___ Concern about being arrested
___ Concern about becoming addicted
___ Conflict with my beliefs
___ Concern about loss of energy or ambition
___ Concern about possible loss of self-control
___ Possibility that marijuana use might lead to use of stronger drugs
___ Unenjoyable experience
___ Disapproval of my parents
___ Disapproval of my boyfriend/girlfriend
___ Pressure from my friends who don't use it
___ Possibility of a bad trip
___ High cost
___ Unavailability
___ No urge to get high

22. During what time of the year would you say that students in your school are most likely to use alcohol or other drugs?

___ Summer
___ Fall, after the school year begins
___ Christmas vacation
___ Winter
___ Spring, near the end of the school year
___ Don't believe students in my school use alcohol or other drugs

The following set of answers can be used for questions 23 through 30.

___ None
___ One
___ Two
___ Three
___ Four or more

23. During the past 12 months, how many times have you received a ticket or been stopped and warned for a moving violation such as speeding, running a stoplight, or improper passing?
24. How many of these tickets or warnings did you receive after you had been drinking alcohol?
25. How many of these tickets or warnings did you receive after you had been smoking marijuana or hashish?
26. How many of these tickets or warnings did you receive after you had been using other drugs?
27. During the past 12 months, how many accidents have you had while you were driving a car, truck, or motorcycle, whether or not you were responsible? (An accident means a collision involving property damage and/or personal injury. It does not mean bumps or scratches in parking lots.)
28. How many of these accidents occurred after you had been drinking alcohol?
29. How many of these accidents occurred after you had been smoking marijuana or hashish?
30. How many of these accidents occurred after you had been using other drugs?
31. Do you think any member of your immediate family (father, mother, brother, or sister) now has a drug or alcohol problem?

    ____ Yes
    ____ Maybe
    ____ No
    ____ Don't know

32. If you had a question or concern about alcohol or other drugs, would you talk to your parents or guardians?

    ____ Definitely not
    ____ Maybe
    ____ Probably
    ____ Definitely yes

33. If you had a problem with alcohol or other drugs, who would you most likely ask for help or advice? (Check one answer only.)

　―― My parents
　―― A friend my own age
　―― A relative (aunt, uncle, brother, or sister)
　―― A priest, minister, or rabbi
　―― A coach
　―― A teacher or counselor at school
　―― A counselor who does not work at my school
　―― No one

APPENDIX C

Sample Form for Needs Assessment Interview

Using these questions, you can gather information about an individual's perceptions of the magnitude of the drug and alcohol problem in the community. You also can learn how this problem affects the community in general and this individual in particular.

1. What are your general impressions regarding the extent of drug and alcohol use by young people (age 18 and under) in this community?

2. With what age-group and in what type of agency do you work? How many clients in this age-group make up your caseload? (If the interviewee does not work for an agency, you can ask how many young people he or she deals with on a regular basis.)

3. Of the young people with whom you work regularly, what percentage do you think are having problems related to the use of alcohol? Marijuana? Any other drug?

4. Which of the following problems do you see in the young people you suspect of using alcohol and/or other drugs?

    ____ Truancy/absenteeism/tardiness
    ____ Poor academic performance
    ____ Behavior warranting disciplinary action by the school
    ____ Reckless driving
    ____ Illegal activity directly related to the buying or selling of drugs

___ Illegal activity not directly related to drug use, for example, vandalism, burglary
___ Disruption of family life, for example, arguments, curfew violations, lack of cooperation
___ Other (please specify) ———————————

5. How many of the young people with whom you work regularly have problems related to their parents' use of alcohol and/or other drugs? What kinds of problems?

6. Can you describe in more detail two or three young people who are having some of the problems you just specified? Mention those that immediately come to mind or that affect you most profoundly.

7. Where and from whom do you think young people obtain the chemicals they use?

8. When and where do you believe young people usually use alcohol and/or other drugs?

9. Do you think the adults in this community recognize that we have an adolescent drug problem?

10. What do you believe the adults in this community think about this issue?

11. What do you think this community can do about adolescent drug and alcohol use and abuse?

12. Would you be willing to relate your information and experiences to people attending a special school board (or county commissioners, hospital board, court services board, task force) meeting?

APPENDIX D

Sample Information Form on Service Providers

These general questions can help you gather relevant information about local service providers. If a particular provider does not already offer services to people who have drug-related problems, you may wish to ask about its willingness to provide such services in the future.

Name of provider _____

Address _____ Telephone number _____

_____ Business hours _____

_____

Director _____ Person contacted _____

Date opened _____ Date of contact _____

Population served _____

Sliding fee scale and/or fee structure _____

Insurance coverage _____

Government support _____ Private funding _____

List name, title, position, and academic degree(s) of staff members.

Briefly describe physical facilities.

Briefly describe location, parking facilities, bus service.

Briefly describe intake procedures.

Describe confidentiality policy as it pertains to adolescents and adults.

Describe policy regarding the sharing of information with person or agency making referral.

List specific individual and group services offered.

Describe philosophy regarding clients' alcohol and drug use.

References ───────────────────────────

APPENDIX E

Sample Program Proposal Outline

You may use this sample outline if the governing body that you are approaching does not prefer another proposal format. Omit, expand, or streamline the sections to suit your needs.

I. Background
   A. Brief description of task force
      1. Reason(s) for forming interest group
      2. Reasons for converting interest group to task force
      3. Significant dates in task force development
   B. Task force members
      1. Name, occupation
      2. Task force duty
      3. Reason for joining task force

II. General definition of adolescent drug problem
   A. National, state, regional, and/or local statistics
      1. Drug use among adolescents
      2. Alcohol consumption among adolescents
      3. Other persuasive information
   B. Current trends in adolescent drug use
      1. Earlier age of first use
      2. Increase in use of alcohol and other drugs
      3. Increase of drunkenness and overdosing
      4. Correlation between use of alcohol and use of other drugs

  C. Problems associated with acute intoxication and overdosing
    1. Highway accidents
    2. Blackouts
    3. Suicides
    4. Attempted suicides
    5. Unlawful behavior
  D. Issues concerning children of alcoholics
    1. Low self-esteem, guilt, and shame
    2. High risk of chemical dependency
    3. Predictable patterns of destructive behavior
III. Local needs assessment
  A. Results of survey of adolescent drug use patterns
  B. Information gained from interviews of key persons detailing how adolescent drug use affects:
    1. Family life
    2. Health, growth, and development
    3. Schools
    4. Juvenile justice system
    5. Community at large
IV. Early-intervention program goals
  A. Definition of goals in relation to:
    1. Young people
    2. Parents
    3. System staff members
    4. Community at large
  B. Means of achieving goals
    1. Awareness and education presentations
    2. Identification and referral services
    3. Continuum of counseling and treatment services
    4. Support groups and activities
V. Organizational considerations
  A. Placement of early-intervention program within system
  B. Relationship to other programs within system

VI. Sequence of program implementation
   A. Policies
      1. Drafting or revision completed by _____ (date)
      2. Suggested date for implementation
   B. Procedures
      1. Drafting or revision completed by _____ (date)
      2. Suggested date for implementation
   C. Services
      1. Preliminary assessment procedures
      2. Specific groups
      3. Awareness and education programs
      4. In-service training of system staff members

VII. Staffing
   A. Program coordinator
      1. Rationale
      2. Job description
      3. Qualifications
   B. Advisory board
      1. Members (list them)
      2. Responsibilities
   C. Core team
      1. Present members (list them)
      2. Projected number of additional members needed
      3. Qualifications
      4. Present positions within system
      5. Program-related duties
      6. Training
      7. Date of team formation, if team does not already exist

VIII. Program costs and funding plans
   A. Coordinator's salary
   B. Other expenses
      1. Publications
      2. Materials
      3. Training

C. Funding considerations
   1. Budget allotment
   2. Donations
   3. Matching funds
IX. Program evaluation
   A. Two-year commitment on part of governing body to program development and implementation
   B. Evaluation procedures developed by _____ (date)
   C. Evaluation done by task force members (list them)
   D. Results of evaluation to be reported to governing body by _____ (date)

APPENDIX F

References

Chapter One

1. Johnston L., Bachman J., O'Malley P. *Highlights from Student Drug Use in America 1975-1981*. Rockville, Maryland: National Institute on Drug Abuse, Division of Research, 1982. p. 54.
2. Ibid., p. 53.
3. Borton T., ed. "Pressure to Try Drugs, Alcohol Starts in Early Grades, Survey Shows," *Weekly Reader*. Middletown, Connecticut: Xerox Education Publications, April 25, 1983.
4. Rachal J., Guess L., Hubbard R., et al. "Facts for Planning, No. 4: Alcohol Misuse by Adolescents," *Facts for Planning: Alcohol and Youth*. Washington, D.C.: National Institute on Alcohol Abuse and Alcoholism, 1982. p. 62.
5. Lowman C. "Facts for Planning, No. 7: Drinking and Driving Among Youth," *Alcohol Health and Research World*. Vol. 7, No. 2, Winter 1982/83. p. 42.
6. Lerner R. "Schools Can Provide Drug Abuse Prevention Tools," *Focus on Alcohol and Drug Issues*. 6(2):22-23, 1983.
7. Nammakal S. "Student Drug Survey, Minnetonka School District." Minnetonka, Minnesota, January 1981.
8. Muldoon J. "Police Go Undercover in Nation's High Schools," *Community Intervention Newsletter*. Minneapolis: Community Intervention, Inc., Fall 1981. p. 5.

Chapter Three

1. Johnston L., Bachman J., O'Malley P. *Student Drug Use in America 1975-1981*. Rockville, Maryland: National Institute on Drug Abuse, Division of Research, 1981. p. 283.

About the Author

James F. Crowley is president of Community Intervention, Inc., a Minneapolis-based consulting, training, and publishing organization.

During Community Intervention's ten-year history, communities across the country have been assisted in developing strategic, effective, and community-based programs that address youth, alcohol, and drug issues.

Mr. Crowley earned a master's degree from the College of St. Thomas, St. Paul, Minnesota, and has ten years of teaching and administrative experience in both public and private schools. He has fifteen years of experience in training, program consultation, and program administration in the field of chemical dependency and has given hundreds of presentations to community groups and national audiences. He is co-author of *The Alliance for Change Task Force Planning Guide, One Step Ahead: Early Intervention Strategies for Teenage Drug Problems,* and *Effective Student Assistance Programs.*

About Community Intervention

Community Intervention, Inc., is a Minneapolis, Minnesota, based training, consulting, and publishing organization. For the past ten years, they have worked with communities across the country to develop strategic, effective, and community-based programs that address youth, alcohol and drug issues.

In addition to offering services that deal with drugs, Community Intervention also offers support and expertise for other issues that negatively impact youth, such as suicide, eating disorders, and child abuse.

Community Intervention utilizes the talents of more than 60 professionals to teach and consult with communities dealing with youth issues. This staff has direct experience and skills in: alcohol/drug treatment, drug prevention, community mobilization, law enforcement, student assistance programming, family therapy, juvenile probation, and other related areas. The staff's practical skills and experience provide Community Intervention with the range and flexibility to meet local programming needs.